The Battle Scarred Guide to Small Business Debt Relief and Recovery

BookSurge Publishing
North Charleston, South Carolina 29418
www.booksurge.com

Thomson, Ken
The Battle-Scarred Guide to Small Business Debt Relief and Recovery
1. Small business—Management.
2. New business enterprises—Management.
3. Success in business
Printed in the United States of America
10 9 8 7 6 5 4 3 2 1

Editor: David Congdon
Cover design by
www.Eight-Eleven.com

The Battle Scarred Guide to Small Business Debt Relief and Recovery

No-nonsense, spill the beans lessons from a turnaround professional

Ken Thomson

Edited by David Congdon

BookSurge
Publishing
2008

The Battle Scarred Guide to Small Business Debt Relief and Recovery

TABLE OF CONTENTS

This book is dedicated to my beloved wife, Elisabeth,
who has stuck with me through thick and thin,
produced two wonderful sons and, as ever,
keeps me on an even keel.

INTRODUCTION

Business success stories make great news copy. After all, the American dream is to own your own company and sell it for millions when the time is ripe. But we are often blind to the fact that the vast majority of new firms fail within five years. US Small Business Administration (SBA) figures bear this out.

Despite your initial enthusiasm, you will likely have to navigate your company through troubled financial waters sooner than later. It can be devastating to run out of cash if you are unprepared, but if it can happen to large established firms—which it does—it can certainly happen to yours. This is often the tipping point that forces people out of business.

This book is designed to improve your odds for success, with little known but battle-tested strategies to manage your business realistically and protect it from danger.

Well defined processes are laid out to make you and your company more resilient. Amongst other things, you are shown practical steps to build your business credit, to wean you off reliance on your own. You also discover how to protect your corporate and personal assets from the potential ravages of creditors and their lawsuits. And of crucial importance, you get insight on how to ramp up your marketing, to bring in the extra revenues that you need.

It is understood that you may be reading this book solely for the information in Part One, on how to immediately take action to tackle crushing debt. But the systems and strategies outlined in Part Two are important as they make it easier for a company to survive a cash flow crisis. If corporate and personal assets are exposed to creditor lawsuits, for example, it can be more challenging to get the debt reduction and restructuring you may need to save your company.

You find out in Part One how to fight problem debt. You are given the specifics on how to buy time with creditors, work your way out of trouble, settle this debt for cents on the dollar and negotiate lower monthly carrying costs for secured loans. And, if you eventually have to bale out, you are shown a private and perfectly legal maneuver to let you keep your business assets and start afresh, while leaving behind the old debt that was holding you back.

This practical information comes from many years of professional experience in turning around the fortunes of hundreds of troubled businesses. The process of doing so is not widely understood. For example, few attorneys or accountants will show you how to get out of trouble by settling debt for cents on the dollar. It's just not part of their education or mindset.

Most of us learn from our own mistakes—or at least, we should. Some of the lessons in this book are derived from my first learning what not to do. My own first business venture lasted three years and died a sad and lingering death, taking our family house with it. I've also learned from the mistakes made by others—clients of my business turnaround firm. In most cases, after taking the steps outlined here, they have profited from the trial by fire, to become the successful firms they were meant to be in the first place.

If you want to build a resilient money machine, free of the debt problems faced by so many entrepreneurs, then the information provided here will help you get there.

A final but important note relates to the use of gender. It would be cumbersome to use such terminology as "She or He," or "Her or Him." Regretfully, I had to choose the traditional convention of using "he" and "him." This is ironic, because the growth in companies founded by women in this country far outstrips those started and managed by men. I trust that my rationale is understood and acceptable to all.

PART ONE

Beat the Survival Odds—Tackle Crushing Debt

1

Adopt a Positive Debt-Fighting Attitude

Your first sign of trouble is an insistent call from a creditor, whose receivable is ninety days overdue. Then another calls. The bank asks if you can cover a check. Eventually, the phone rings off the hook. Your receptionist starts looking for other employment and you can't think of what to do to turn this around.

You are not alone. This scenario repeats itself in many thousands of American companies every day. The question is, are you in the right frame of mind to handle it?

Obviously, debt represents a fundamental obligation to do everything possible to honor the commitment another firm has made to yours, by supplying goods or services, for which you promised to pay. As an honest individual, you want to make sure that your firm responds in a way in which this trust is honored. But you may have to remind yourself that past-due problem debt has everything to do with the risk inherent in being in business and little to do with your personal character, or that of other managers in your company.

Officers of large privately held or public companies know this. For example, it was readily understood that the legacy US airline carriers became crippled by the increased competition from low-priced operators, higher fuel prices, the aftermath of the 9/11 attacks and other factors. Few would claim that the airlines' management lacked moral standing. Their problems were risk-based, due to business factors. The same applies to the negative financial issues faced by most small to medium sized businesses.

Bankruptcy attorneys' eyes shine brightly when retained to divest debt in a Chapter 11 reorganization filing. Do they become emotionally involved and disturbed about the financial impact on creditors of their substantial fees? I don't think so.

Our attitudes toward bad debt derive from colonial times and beyond. As recently as the immediate post-Revolutionary period, debtors were routinely thrown into jail. They were not fed or clothed by the authorities. Instead, reliance was placed on whatever could be accessed from sympathetic parties outside, such as family and the Humane Society.

So hostile was the prevailing attitude that, when Yellow Fever swept through Philadelphia in 1798, the prison population was moved to safety outside of the City. All, that is, except the debtors who, shamed and mistrusted, had to stay and endure horrific conditions.

Thomas Rodney, an officer of the Revolution, member of the Continental Congress and Judge of the Supreme Court of Delaware, served time in debtor's prison, as did countless other notables. A horseback-mounted statue of Rodney's older brother, Caesar, signer of the Declaration of Independence, stands proudly in Rodney Square, Wilmington, Delaware. Ironically, it overlooks the former corporate offices of credit card behemoth, MBNA, absorbed in 2006 by the Bank of America. He seems ready to jump his steed off the plinth and charge headlong through its front entrance.

It was not until enactment of The 1800 Bankruptcy Act, aimed at elite commercial debtors, that new perspectives began to emerge on a national level. But it took almost a century, until 1898, for bankruptcy law to become a permanent part of the federal system.

Commercial insolvency has long been perceived as an economic issue and part of the risk of doing business. And it is separated from the concepts of morality and impropriety that had traditionally and unfairly been associated with bad consumer debt. Even so, managers of small to medium sized companies in financial hot water often tend to personalize the problem. They get into "debt-denial." This can hurt their ability to take effective action. And of course, the terminology used doesn't help. Terms such as "delinquent," "failure" and "deadbeat" spring to mind. Collectors often thrive on this vernacular. It strikes a raw nerve, which is why some of them use it. And it works when they are dealing with the unprepared.

Your firm may have a serious and protracted cash crunch to deal with. Persistent phone calls from creditors and their agents may leave you and your staff disturbed and alarmed. But you cannot fall into the trap where you personalize the debt and become paralyzed by guilt and remorse. This serves you and your company no good. Specific and realistic options are available to you, as described in following chapters, to help get your firm out of trouble.

You deserve to work through this situation to preserve your business and, to the extent possible, to honor the needs of your creditors. You want to do the best for them that you can. But it is of no use to anyone if your concerns for their welfare end up with your firm going out of business.

Use the same mindset as that of a Fortune 500 company CEO. Your primary responsibility is to your team and investors and the continuing survival of your organization. The immediate needs of creditors are, of brutal necessity, secondary to this.

Summary
1.   Understand that you have an obligation to meet

the needs of your company's creditors to the best of your abilities, consistent with your own survival.

2. This is an economic problem, associated with the risk of doing business. It has nothing to do with your character as a business owner or officer, if you and your management team are doing everything possible to minimize the damage.

3. If you ignore the problem, it will put you out of business. Get into the right frame of mind to take immediate action to fix it, as outlined in following chapters.

Lesson

Think like the CEO of a large company—protect your firm at all costs.

Note

For a witty and thoroughly readable history of debt and bankruptcy in the age of American Independence, see 'Republic of Debtors' by Bruce H. Mann. (Harvard University Press, 2002).

2

Control Worry—or it will Control You

We live in a society where entrepreneurs are seen to be fiercely individualistic. And we are. But that does not mean to say that we don't worry or need counsel and advice when things get tough. In fact, there's an exclusive organization most of us belong to. It's called the Club of Fear.

Ask anyone who's been in business for a few years. Most will admit that they have gone through very tough times. It comes with the territory. What makes it worse is that most think they're alone in this. But a huge percentage of businesses fold their tents by their fifth year. This represents countless owners who jolt themselves awake in the middle of the night, worried about lost savings and how to handle the evolving disaster. Families sometimes split apart at this point, which can be another issue to deal with.

The psychological free-fall between rabid enthusiasm and abject terror can be fast and devastating. And there is no government support or unemployment insurance for people who just lost their business.

The problem is often that business people in financial trouble feel that they are alone. Looking around, they can see business success stories everywhere. The newspaper, TV and web are full of them. But we rarely hear of those who are living lives of quiet desperation, struggling to meet payroll and basic costs, wondering how to bring in revenues to stem the tide. Hopelessness sets in when you don't know what to do about it.

Stress and worry stem from not being able to figure out a

way to forge ahead to meet your company's goals. Knowledge and business savvy is power. A lack of this essential ingredient so often hampers a company from working its way out of trouble.

Practical steps to calm creditors down and buy breathing space are laid out in later chapters. Once this has been done, and assuming you have done everything possible to cut costs, you have to concentrate on a strategy to improve revenues.

No other function is as important as the ability to revise your marketing plan to improve your top line. This may sound obvious, but productive changes can often be quite simple. I have dealt with many companies that had tried to struggle through without improving their marketing. And the consequent failure to increase revenues leads to a downward spiral of more worry and stress.

It is really hard to describe to someone the raw fear that goes through a person's mind when they have a sick company, unless they've been through it themselves. I'm speaking from experience. I had invested all our savings in our first business venture—a specialty retail store. Marketing research and media coverage pointed to infinite demand for our merchandise. Everything looked great. We had a solid business plan and— we thought—adequate capital reserves. But a major recession soon cut consumer demand. Our moderate sales projections went in the tank. And my over-optimistic approach had led me into a long-term property lease. The landlord had us all tied up with nowhere to go.

The company bled its precious capital while we tried to get our marketing turned around. But it was a tough sell. Eventually, three years later, we got out, wiser and temporarily poorer. I always consider that experience to be a trial by fire. I've at least got the right to discuss entrepreneurial stress and worry as someone who has gone through it and survived, then thrived. While we can laugh at it in hindsight, it was a terrifying experience to go through.

I believe that there is truth in Norman Vincent Peale's dictum, "Every adversity contains the seed of an equal or greater benefit." It certainly applied to us and to many others, but it is hard to convey that philosophy to someone in the midst of business trouble. My own recipe to keep worry away is to get on top of problems and act positively to address issues when they come up.

Take the initiative in dealing with business worries. Don't let the underlying concern sap your strength. If your cash flow is inadequate to keep current with payables, what is the root cause? It is likely easier to establish the cause than to fix the problem, but perhaps not. Then you have to come up with alternative solutions and a planned course of action.

We suggest here a strategy to reduce your debt to give you the time and opportunity to get back on track with your marketing plan. At the same time we show how to use cheap and effective tactics to immediately boost revenues.

This advice can fall on deaf ears. Aggressive collectors and other issues at this difficult time can traumatize people and cause them to simply give up, especially if this is a new experience for them. This can be an expensive mistake. It would be far better to face the problems squarely and establish the best option available to address them.

Good advice is to enlist the help of a trusted business coach or advisor—or your advisory board, if you have one—to put into perspective what you are going through. You will conquer worry and stress by figuring out what action to take, with the help of someone who has been there.

Once you have decided on a course of action, pursue it aggressively, even if it is to go out of business. Do it properly, to protect as much of your capital as possible. And remember, you are not the only member of the Club of Fear—far from it. If this is your first time, you are merely paying your entrepreneurial dues. And in future years, you can brag about it.

Summary
1. Worry and stress is a part of being in business. If it develops into sheer terror, join the Club.
2. Get help from others, who can help you identify and remedy the problem, after reviewing options.

Lesson
Be proactive and don't let worry get the better of you.

3

The Seven Deadly Debt Management Sins

As we have discussed, you know you're in trouble when the phone starts to fly off the hook with incoming collection calls. Your receptionist and accounting clerk become desperate. You're too busy doing what it takes to generate revenues to devote time and energy to deal with angry collectors. And when you do talk to them, their threats and accusations leave you shaken.

If times have been good, you may feel especially unprepared to handle a cash flow crisis. The right mental attitude and a commitment to deal effectively and honestly with creditors goes a long way. If I have to list the biggest mistakes I've seen business people make when they get into financial hot water, the following have to be the fatal seven:

1. Debt denial

Don't bury your head in the sand. Too many business people "forget" that they have serious issues to deal with. They're served with a lawsuit? It goes in the bottom drawer, forgotten until the sheriff arrives at the door, gun on hip and clipboard in hand. Or they "forget" to deal with the other unpleasant reminders that they have cash flow problems.

The toughest job of all is sometimes to realize that you have to change course in order to muscle your way through the new realities that challenge your business and your livelihood.

2. Failure to prioritize debts

Some debts can be put on the back burner. Others have to be kept fairly current. Get too far behind in your building lease commitments and the landlord may file suit. And these matters generally get on the fast-track court schedule. Equipment leases can usually be given lesser priority. Unsecured debts for trade and professional services—unfortunately for the supplier—normally get the lowest priority. You want to pay everyone on schedule but, if you cannot, you have to protect your company.

3. Not treating creditors with courtesy

It is easy to say the wrong thing to your creditor in times of stress. It is in your best interests not to let these matters get "personal." Certainly, if a valued supplier calls you, take or return the call. A personal letter can set the scene for an amicable settlement on terms to meet your needs. Many individual payable issues get to court because of personal slights and hostile encounters. It becomes a matter of 'pride' and 'principle'. Don't let that happen to you.

4. Getting spooked by collectors

Commercial debt collectors don't have to abide by the restrained conduct required under federal legislation for those going after individuals. Many are reasonable, but some can be downright obnoxious. This is a time when you are least able to think rationally about your commitments. Don't promise the impossible when under pressure. You have to put together and execute a debt management plan, designed to meet your own business goals and help you stay solvent. Then deal with collectors within that framework.

Collectors work on a commission basis in a confrontational environment and couldn't care less about your business survival. Some will say anything to get you to give them a payment. Don't jump to their tune and make promises and commitments you can't keep, just because they threaten and scream at you and your staff. Knowledge is power. Recognize their motivations and limitations and work within your plan.

5. Making debt payments in the absence of a written settlement agreement

If you are struggling and a collector calls, don't provide a partial payment unless it falls within the framework of an overall settlement agreement. It makes no sense and is of no help to you to send off a payment for a portion of the debt, when you are likely to get hounded again as soon as the check clears.

6. Becoming paralyzed by thoughts of ruined business credit

Many business owners are petrified over losing their "good" Dun & Bradstreet rating if they attempt to negotiate settlements with creditors. But it's not that important in the short term. This statement may seem absurd, because good business credit, and a good reputation, is essential. It certainly is in the long haul. But if you are late with your payables, or if there have been suits or judgments filed, this and other information will already have been listed on your D&B report and elsewhere.

Anyone can access that for the requisite fee. The proactive steps that you take to get out of your tough financial predicament will have a better impact on your business credit than continually trying to muddle through. And if you do nothing, notification of unsatisfied judgments on your D&B report will be far worse.

7. Thinking that bankruptcy or closing the doors is your only option

Many companies close down because their owners simply give up. They receive bad advice or become dejected, and everyone loses out. Sometimes, of course, it's the only answer. A myriad of factors can come into play to cause your problems. But the fact is, unsecured creditors can lose everything if you go out of business. And you can go down with the ship too, if your personal assets are tied to it.

It is often far better to stay alive by reducing and restructuring your debt. It can be in your creditors' best interests to settle for a fraction of that owed, possibly paid over time, to help your firm recover and to reimburse them for at least part of their investment in it. But they won't work with you unless you tell them the facts. And to do that effectively, it is best to provide them with a well-prepared settlement proposal.

Have you ever lost out completely on getting paid because the debtor filed bankruptcy or simply closed its doors? Would you not rather have received a partial payment, or payments, to minimize your losses and possibly retain a customer into the future? Most of us would answer with a resounding "yes", given enough time and information to make a decision. Put yourself in the place of your creditors. Treat them as you would wish to be treated yourself. After reading this book, if you or your team are still unable to take steps to settle these problem debts in a way that meets your company's goals, get professional help. Then get cracking with your business turnaround.

Summary

1. Don't commit these seven deadly sins when your company gets into trouble with problem debt.

2. Communicate well and treat your creditors with the respect they deserve. This will help you to meet your company's goals.

Lesson

Communicate effectively with your firm's creditors, to each party's benefit.

4

Find Extra Cash in a Hurry

Cash flow is King. It is your company's lifeblood. Your business will fail if it runs out, so it stands to reason that you have to know your cash balance at any time. And you absolutely have to be able to make the best projections possible over the next few months. You can't run your business properly without them.

As we have discussed, a huge majority of businesses go under before their fifth year. Even worse, according to Michael Gerber, author of the "The E-Myth Revisited: Why Most Small Businesses Don't Work and What to Do About It", forty percent fail within the first twelve months.

Lots of fancy rationale and opinion is given as to why businesses fold. But the simple fact is that, for whatever reason, they run out of cash. If you get into trouble and want to beat the odds, you have to commit to doing whatever it takes to maintain a positive cash balance. As the saying goes, "If you're up to your ass in alligators, you're not concerned about clearing the swamp." You have to kill the beasts, which means raising cash, before you can take steps to fundamentally improve your business.

Many new businesses owners come to realize that they didn't plan for adequate capital required to get them through the start-up period. When you combine this with a mistaken estimate of market demand and an inability to effectively market your product or services, it is tough knowing how to proceed. How do you get the required cash together to beat back creditors and keep going?

It often requires a small upswing in revenues to make all the difference. But how do you do it? And how long will it take?

My own experience in dealing with companies in trouble is that there is often a high monthly cost structure in place. The commercial lease is too high. The space is too big. The equipment and supplies are too expensive. Sometimes there are too many employees. And frequently, the owner is driving a luxury car, for which the carrying cost of the lease becomes an increasing burden. In fact, there seems to be an inverse relationship between the financial health of the company and the cost of the car.

Vehicles are marketed to us to convey strong impressions about success. Just look at the advertising for luxury cars. It can be very difficult for individuals faced with tough times to divest themselves of a fancy vehicle. Some deep psychological need tells them that they can make cuts elsewhere, but they need this symbol of success to maintain their sense of worth. Unfortunately, creditors' sales people who visit with you will be impressed with your luxuries, too. This can make it very difficult to get their cooperation when you ask for extra time or revised payment terms.

An example of this is painful to me. I was in the process of negotiating a series of sweet deals for a firm in desperate shape. The first one, for a specific creditor, was to be inked at the eleventh hour, at a small-town Pennsylvania courthouse. It was one of these buildings where parking is immediately in front of the courthouse steps.

I arrived early, just before the plaintiff and his attorney drove up in very modest cars. The creditor, especially, had a beaten up domestic vehicle of uncertain age. Standing outside in the morning sunlight, we agreed to dispense with the formalities as soon as my client turned up. To my horror, he arrived in a magnificent, large, late-model Audi. Without putting a fine point on it, he screwed himself. The attorney marched into court and got his judgment.

The moral of the story is, don't send the wrong messages to your creditors.

Twenty Steps to Find Extra Cash in a Hurry

We will discuss in following chapters how to buy time and cut deals with creditors. This gives you the opportunity to make the necessary adjustments to bring in a stronger net cash flow and to build a "war chest" to deal with trade debt. But what do you do right now, as a part of your emergency plan, to find extra cash, either by raising it or cutting your cash outflow? Here are twenty suggestions:

1. Bump your sales revenue

What is your most profitable product or service? Who are your best customers? Focus your marketing on them, to bring in more cash. Chapter 12 covers this in more depth.

Can you sell on-line, if you are not doing so already? Are you capturing customer e-mail addresses to inform them of special offers? Are there other products you can sell on line? The small garage that services our cars could use more business. So it now captures customer email addresses. It informs them of oil change and service specials and other promotions. This has an immediate impact on the bottom line.

The sky's the limit with targeted email marketing to your customer base.

2. Sell unused assets

Many companies have unused and idle equipment lying around. An electrical contractor I worked with raised over $15,000 on Ebay, selling unused and unneeded inventory. CraigsList.org, another on-line resource, can also be used for local sales in most parts of the country.

There is a market for all kinds of office and specialty equipment. Check out what you have, to be disposed of. You might be surprised what you can get for it.

3. Sell hidden assets

Do you have an intangible to sell, such as a product or service that can be marketed by another company? How about associate marketing, where another firm will go to bat to sell your product for a percentage of the gross? That's how information is sold and, in fact, one of the ways in which this book is being marketed.

4. Factor Receivables

Factoring is a way in which you receive cash payment for specific approved receivables. You normally get about seventy percent up front, within several days. Later, when your customer pays the factoring firm, you receive the balance, less its fee of around four percent of the face value.

A few problems arise in a tight cash turnaround situation. Factoring companies typically prefer repeat business and are not generally inclined to do one-off deals. As well, you want to buy time from your creditors for several months. As any particular receivable is expected to come in within thirty to sixty days, it might be better to wait for it to arrive, unless you are truly stuck for cash. After all, you will need the funds to get through the next three months or more. On the other hand, if you are dealing with a big account, a few weeks of non-payment can make the difference between staying in business or not.

Check the web for factors that do this kind of one-off business. The Commercial Finance Association has a request page on CFA.com for every specific type of situation you can imagine.

5. Collect your Receivables

You cannot let debtor firms drive you out of business. I have seen this happen all too often, especially when one or two significant receivables were involved.

My own preference is to get results by communicating clearly and effectively with the other side. Talk turkey and find out the reason for the non-payment. Unless the debtor firm is evasive, you should do everything to help resolve the situation at this stage. If they can't cut a check today, get their commitment to do so within three or four days.

A process is described in Chapter 16 on how to get paid in a conciliatory, non-threatening manner. If your customer absolutely can't pay you in these terms, level with them. These aren't normal times. Your firm is cash starved and they are increasing the pain.

If you still get nowhere, and you are sure you're being taken, assign the account to a good collection attorney. These people generally receive a contingency fee of one-third of the sum they collect, plus court costs. And they don't stop with a judgment. They specialize in actually collecting money, so they take the additional steps to get you paid. After all, unless you get paid, they don't get their cut.

At this crucial stage, you cannot afford to place the account in the hands of a collector. Ensure that the matter proceeds to court forthwith, without due ceremony. This generally gets the other side's attention and—hopefully—you get paid in short order.

6. Tighten your credit policies

Do you know where you stand with your receivables? One plumbing contractor company I worked with was in terrible trouble. Cash flow was in the tank. It couldn't pay its bills. It didn't take long to discover that the accounting clerk was in hospital and no invoices had been sent out for two months!

Suggest small discounts for COD terms to specific customers. Keep on top of late payers. Remind them at the time of re-ordering that you anticipate prompt payment and, again, will give a small discount for their cooperation.

7. Raise prices

You have good products or services? Raise your prices. This might seem counter-intuitive. But if you add value to your offering, price is of lesser concern. You're unlikely to be a gas station on a corner with three other firms, where price is uppermost on the minds of customers.

Once again, using the service station analogy, increase the cost of service by a few percentage points, but do something special in return. Would a free tire rotation cost you more than a few minutes of labor, when the vehicle is already on the hoist?

8. Rent unused space

Do you have unused space that you can lease, or sub-lease? Many companies anticipate the need for more space than needed. Can you partition it off, for use by another business?

Offer a discount for an up-front cash deal. Advertise in CraigsList.org if you are in one of the areas it serves and put an ad in the business section of the local newspaper.

9. Negotiate a property lease reduction.

What would it mean to your landlord if you went out of business? Even if he has you tied up with personal guarantees and a long-term lease, what would he lose? Are potential tenants knocking on his door? Make him an offer, after thoroughly reviewing your situation with him. Done right, there's a good chance that he will see the situation from your perspective. This process is discussed more fully in Chapter 5.

I was astonished, in 1995, to lose out on a potential negotiated settlement for rent reduction of an Irish restaurant and pub. It was a stand-alone location. The landlord was adamant. Although he had no other candidates for the space, he was determined to keep the original terms of the lease. He had taken my client to court and eventually threw him out. Thirteen years later, the building still stands unoccupied. It was truly a lose-lose situation, engineered by a bone-headed property owner.

This situation was unusual and the exception that proves the rule. Don't be afraid to talk to your landlord about a rent reduction. Be clear about your situation. Make it in his best interests to come around to your point of view.

10. Get equity from a sale and leaseback

Do you own your own building? Talk to a realtor to see if there is a buyer for the property. A printer client did this to save his business. He planned to sell the company within five years, after getting help to raise its value by improving systems and boosting revenues. The firm next door had made inquiries. It purchased the building for expansion, but agreed to wait out his planned exit.

11. Get better terms in your purchasing

Check the web for better deals. Question the costs on whatever you buy. Negotiate with everyone. Are you better switching to other services? How about telephones? Could you use a web-based service, such as Vonage?

12. Call in the expense reduction experts.

Put your overhead under a microscope and start saving. Companies are available to do contingency-based audits on the utilities and other services you already purchase. They get paid as a percentage of your savings, so they are committed to get results for you.

Utilitech.com is a veteran-owned firm that conducts utility and telecommunication audits. IntegrityBusinessPartners.com is another good firm. Other specialists are available to help you save money on office supplies, trash, freight and other overheads.

13. Cut Payroll

You're in a bind. You want to keep key people in a competitive environment, but the business needs to survive. Do the best you can for these individuals.

The quickest and most effective way to cut costs is to focus on unproductive and replaceable staff. You have to let them go in a crisis. Also, look at overtime. A sign company I worked with was able to make huge improvements just by cutting overtime. Staff in this labor-intensive business had come to expect the extra hours and become less efficient at finishing projects during regular work time. The change was sold to them as a way of keeping their jobs.

14. Cancel all wasteful perks

Substitute video- and teleconferencing for business trips. Totally cut non-essential expenses. No expensive restaurant meals. The company needs cash. Cut expense account costs. Ask staff to be creative.

15. Reduce your compensation

Send a message to your staff. Cut your salary and, if you drive a fancy car, get rid of it. If it is leased, Swapalease.com or Leasetrader.com will find somebody to assume it. At the same time, take a cheaper lease from someone else—or better yet, make do with an existing vehicle.

Nothing speaks louder to others than your own personal actions and commitment to change.

16. Refinance and restructure debt

Meet the twin goals of raising cash and bullet-proofing your company from creditors, by financing any asset available, before you get into more serious trouble. You can find specific lenders that specialize in business turnarounds. UCC-1 liens that have been placed to secure asset-based financing will make the assets impossible to attach (seize and sell) by a potential future judgment holder. This bargaining chip will serve you well when negotiating trade settlements later.

Approach your banker to reduce your monthly commitments. This has to be done carefully and methodically and is discussed in Chapter 6.

17. Cut inventory

Don't make bigger orders than necessary. Use web-based just-in-time delivery for office supplies. Don't get carried away by saving a couple of percentage points on volume. Saving cash is the name of the game.

If you have excess inventory that can be returned to the supplier for immediate credit, or sold at a discount, do it.

18. Enlist the help of employees

Establish cost-cutting goals for your company. Challenge

employees to identify any area where a reduction can be made. Let them know their security is on the line. You have got to get through this as a team.

19. Economize in advertising

Is your Yellow Pages and other directory advertising up for renewal? Do you really need all of it? This can be a huge sinkhole for your cash, if the ads don't pull. They work for some industries, but not others.

Direct response is the way to go. Figure out the most cost-effective mix and format to bring in the business.

Is there a better way to promote your business? Are you using the web effectively?

Have you considered writing press releases to provide information and promote your business? If you do this yourself it's free and is covered in Chapter 12.

20. Minimize professional fees

You need good legal help, but use it sparingly. Stay the hell out of court, unless to file answers to debt actions, when you need time to negotiate and settle later. Litigation is outrageously expensive.

An ancient German print in our firm's possession shows two farmers arguing over the ownership of a dairy cow. While one pulls at the poor animal's horns, the other tugs at its tail. (Exhibit #1) An attorney sits in the middle—calmly milking the cow! Nowadays, of course, you would expect to see two legal professionals fully engaged, one representing each party. The caption sensibly advises that it is best to settle your differences amicably. As an aside, and to the great credit of lawyer friends, many have seen the humor in this depiction and have hung copies of the print in their own offices.

Exhibit #1

Settle your differences Amicably and Stay the Hell out of Court

You have to question what your attorney is going to cost your company. There is no question about the value of their routine assistance. But young lawyers will often give better rates than more experienced legal counsel. If the bill seems too high, don't hesitate to question the figures and ask for more detail.

If you retain an attorney to collect money, get a bona fide collection attorney, who will work on a results-based contingency fee. There is no huge up-front fee. In that way, you both want quick results and you know, ahead of time, that the fee will come out of collected funds.

Cut the costs of accountancy. Find a good accountant who will moonlight for you, to make extra money.

Use a workout or debt management professional to reduce and restructure your debt by all means—but only on a fee-for-results, contingency basis. And if you are asked for thirty percent of the savings, or more, it's way too much. Insist on twenty-five per cent, unless there are unusual circumstances to the assignment.

A Final Point—A huge potential cost item that has to be mentioned—shrinkage

I have directly witnessed the traumatic impact of theft in many businesses.

- A crooked employee diverted a Philadelphia hardware store client's goods for many years. He had set up and managed a flea market stand to sell the stolen merchandise.
- A bookkeeper diverted funds from her environmental contractor employer to buy a car and other goods.
- An accountant stole in excess of a million dollars from a vibrant small engineering firm, taking

employee retirement funds and forcing it out of business.

- A transportation firm's accountant embezzled funds for years before absconding, after destroying or removing every financial record he had been involved with.

The fact that all these people served jail time was of no help to the businesses put in jeopardy. This might not happen to you, but beware of theft. Do you <u>really</u> have a tight control on your cash and merchandise?

The four individuals listed here—amongst others I became aware of—were all valued employees. Most of us are naturally trustful. But watch out for theft. Crooks sometimes operate for years before being caught. One might work for you. Opportunists at a time of stress can steal you blind and drive you under.

Summary

1. These are twenty of the most productive ways used by business turnaround professionals to bump revenues and cut costs.

2. You don't necessarily need to use all of them, but you will want to try everything if you are serious about saving your company.

Lesson

Do whatever it takes to bring in extra cash and build a "war chest" to keep your company alive during this critical phase.

5

Dealing with your Landlord

Your property lease payment is likely to be a major cost item. It is often the second largest business expense, after payroll. Anything you can do to reduce it, even temporarily, can be a huge boost to your bottom line.

See the situation from your landlord's eyes. His interests dovetail with yours in more ways than you may think. He also has a business to run and investment to protect, whether or not he is an individual owner or a manager for a large corporate concern. He anticipates a steady stream of revenues from a stable company, but understands that rental income is not an annuity. He knows that business is risky, with bumps in the road. Just look at the statistics. Even major anchor stores in shopping centers can disappear. He likely has direct experience of problems similar to yours.

The biggest mistake tenants can make is to confront and blame the landlord for their troubles. Don't criticize their baby. They won't automatically see it your way. He can't be blamed for your own cash flow problems. He has no control over the economy, or seasonal fluctuations or competitors opening up nearby. As in any negotiation, psychology is important. An aggressive approach is guaranteed to put his back up and hinder your chance for a successful outcome.

The Importance of Timing

Your landlord wields power, but is not a mind reader. He will certainly become concerned if you miss a payment without any prior notice. As in everything, the key is effective communication. Let the landlord or property manager know when trouble looms and when you need help.

This is easier said than done. It may take many calls, letters and emails to get your landlord to take your situation seriously. If he first says "no," you have to be persistent. Don't remain silent. Give him the facts he needs, to show that it is in each party's best interests to come to an alternative agreement on how to proceed.

Dale R. Willerton, president of TheLeaseCoach.com, knows this scenario well. His well-established and successful firm goes to bat for commercial tenants. But before this, he cut his teeth managing leased property, including shopping centers.

In this previous existence, once Dale discovered a tenant to be in financial distress, it was often too late. There had typically been no prior communication. It could take several months and multiple appointments to arrange for the lease termination, if that's what was needed. The landlord's income may have stopped in the meantime. And the time, hassle and expense required to find a new, qualified tenant could be enormous.

It's a fact that the landlord is likely to take your arguments more seriously when you are late, or can only submit partial payments. You will bring him to the table after he realizes that it is in his best interests to help broker a solution. If you could not get his attention when the lease payments were current, you will at least have taken the high road by building your case beforehand. It was no fault of your own if he had turned a deaf ear at the time.

How to proceed with negotiations

You will need to establish your goals at the outset. What kind of reduction do you want, and for how long? Do you want rent relief, or rent abatement? There's a big difference. Your needs will depend on how deep your crisis has become.

1. **Rent relief** is a process of restructuring the payments in such a way that near term payments, in whole or part, are transferred to later in the lease term. Essentially, you pay the same sum over time. You will likely propose this if you are confident that your company is basically sound, but that you need time to get back on track.

2. **Rent abatement** involves paying less than your original contractual obligations. The landlord writes off a portion of the anticipated payments. You will likely ask for this if you are in a tough, protracted crunch and are on shaky ground. You may be able to get rent forgiveness for six months, together with a reduction of twenty percent for the balance of the lease. Or perhaps a fifty percent reduction from this point on.

3. **Get out of the lease** in a way that meets the best interests of both parties.

Your approach will depend on multiple factors impacting your business and the landlord alike. Give some thought to his position:

*   Do you have an interesting business that the landlord would want to keep?
*   Is he actively seeking tenants for other un-rented space?
*   Have other tenants indicated to you that they intend to move out?

- Is there other, more attractive space nearby?

Given your analysis of your own situation, it serves your purposes to document your issues and needs. Compare them with those of your landlord. Put this in writing in the form of a proposal. Obviously, you can't make the monthly lease payments, so discuss the reasons for this:

- Why did your company's abilities change since the lease was signed?
- Explain specifically what happened to cause the poor cash flow, which resulted in your inability to pay full rent
- Provide your analysis of future cash flow, covering the entire lease period.

If you want to stay in the space, your analysis will lead you to the conclusion that your needs are best served by asking for either rent relief or rent abatement. In an extreme case, you may need to move out of the space.

Your meeting with the Landlord

Your best approach is likely to explain your circumstances at the outset and win the landlord around to your way of thinking. Let him understand how the situation has developed. Your proposal is not needed at this stage, unless specifically asked for. You are asking for his input and you don't want to hit him over the head with facts and figures, unless he specifically asks for them.

A gutsy approach is to tell him you are prepared to give the keys back and move out as quickly as possible. If nothing else, he is likely to respond by saying that this is not his wish. Remember that it can take a huge amount of time and money to find a suitable new tenant. He would likely have to renovate the space to suit and generally lose out, big time.

Ask him if he has any suggestions to help you to forge your way through the tough business circumstances that you describe. You might be surprised at his initial feedback. Make the solution to your problem his priority, so that he becomes a proactive force in your recovery. He may come up with some surprisingly helpful suggestions.

If you definitely want out of the lease within a specific timeframe, offer to help locate another tenant. Sign a surrender agreement and do everything possible to make prospective tenants comfortable when viewing the space.

If your business is strong and you are temporarily cash strapped, you might want to discuss a rent relief deal, where you pay nothing for several months, to get on your feet, with a balloon payment at lease end. If you are asked for a personal guarantee, my opinion is to refuse, unless you are absolutely sure that the business will survive. But who can guarantee that? No matter how sure you feel about it, there is always a chance that your business will go under. And if it is tied to your personal fortunes, you could lose your house, too.

Remember that nothing is cast in stone. A balloon payment that you arrange now as part of a rent relief deal can still be negotiated downwards, or completely removed, at the end of the lease period. Your goal is to survive. Do anything you can to make that happen.

If you desperately need help and foresee no other option than rent abatement, bring this up. If it meets your landlord's goal to give you six months, rent-free, he will do it. But you have to ask for it, because it's not going to happen unless you do.

Do you need a lawyer?

You're dealing with a business problem, not a legal problem. It is really up to you. From my perspective, having negotiated many property leases on behalf of business clients—most of which had first reached court—I can vouch for the fact that attorneys are not essential. Some of my best friends are lawyers, but they're not necessarily trained in how to understand business financial issues.

Consider using the services of a group that specializes entirely in helping business people with commercial property lease issues—The Lease Coach. (TheLeaseCoach.com).

Put yourself in the position of your landlord. If you are to turn up with a professional at your side, does he want to see a business specialist or an attorney? I think it's a no-brainer. Don't antagonize or confront your landlord. Take the soft approach. Ask for his help. Then take it from there.

Summary

1. Establish how to match your goals with those of your landlord.
2. Be persistent, if the landlord initially turns a deaf ear. Remember that you can both lose if this is not handled properly.
3. Be conciliatory and ask for your landlord's advice and input. If you need professional help to meet your goals, consider the services of a professional who specializes in commercial lease issues, or in business debt management.

Lesson

Nothing is cast in stone. Communicate effectively with your landlord to get the results you need.

6

Dealing with your Banker

It's tough enough to have cash flow problems, with all that entails. But few things strike more terror into the heart of an entrepreneur than crossing swords with their banker. Even the best of them are risk-averse and don't like surprises, especially when you don't make your monthly payment.

Do you ever look at the advertising that banks put out to compete for your business? They use slogans such as, "We're the banking choice for small business." The trouble is, so often it can feel like they don't have your small business in mind, especially if you want them to go the extra mile for you. The problem can be compounded in a large impersonal bank, where you are unable to get a close, personal relationship with a local loans officer.

As with any negotiation with a large corporation, whether you're discussing a loan or settlement of a trade debt, you have to remember that the people you deal with are small cogs in a big wheel. They have supervisors and probably a committee to report to. Your performance can reflect badly on them, especially if they have gone to bat to get you loan in the first place.

Put yourself in their shoes. Loan officers can be your greatest allies, if dealt with properly. If you get into trouble, be absolutely truthful with them. Put your situation and proposal in writing. Be clear on why you need help and what you want the bank to do. You need the loan officer's superiors—the ultimate decision makers—to read and understand, unfiltered by others, exactly what you propose. Your approach can determine whether it will work with you, or call the loan.

How to proceed

It is clear to both you and the bank when you default on your loan. You will have gone past the grace period—normally ten days—beyond which you will have breached the terms of your agreement. You can also default by not providing the routine information required by your loan agreement. But nothing gets the bank's attention more quickly than an unheralded missed payment.

Your best policy is to let your loan officer know of your situation before you reach the stage that you are about to default. The last thing you need is to become argumentative or ask for more money at this point. This will definitely not help. If you look like you will not be able to meet your commitments, or if this has actually happened, the bank will have lost a certain degree of confidence in your firm. It is not about to dig itself deeper in the hole by giving you more at this point.

After you miss a scheduled payment, the bank can be expected to take whatever checks are deposited in your company's account, to cover the sum due. You may need this for payroll. The importance of an alternative account with another bank is clear at this stage. It can mean the difference between business survival and failure, if you need cash to pay current liabilities.

Clearly, you have to put a basic financial plan together as best you can, for immediate discussion with your loan officer. This is not a time where you can necessarily think straight. You will likely need help from your accountant in order to put this together quickly and effectively.

Your plan will show in detail, with a cash flow forecast and the assumptions used, how you are going to generate the net revenues required to pay the bank.

Your proposed revisions to the terms of the loan will be incorporated into the plan, showing how the bank would still benefit from working with you, if on different terms than those originally agreed to.

Your goal at the meeting

Your objective is to maintain the initiative and show that you are on top of the developing situation. Ask your accountant or business consultant to attend, to further impress the fact that you are truly serious in turning the situation around.

Banks have their own turnaround staff, whose intent is to protect their employer's interests when a customer gets into financial trouble. Depending on the situation, your loan officer may be joined by his manager and one of these people.

You may want interest-only payments for a specific period to get you through, or a grace period of several months. You may also want a restructured loan with lower interest rates. Your request has to match your capabilities, based on past performance and the content of your turnaround plan. Put this in terms of what you can do and leave it to the bank to respond as to what it is willing to offer.

If your figures look positive and you present the plan in a professional manner, the bank will likely be interested in discussing this further. Bankers frequently have to deal with irrational and unwritten requests. Set yourself apart.

Make sure you offer to provide whatever other information that may be needed for the bank to make a decision in your favor.

The bank's menu of choice to help you generally comprises several basic courses of action:

1. Reducing monthly payments, by restructuring the loan, using:
   a. longer amortization period
   b. reduced interest rate
   c. interest-only payments, for a specific time
2. Requesting more collateral from you, to permit it to consider changing the terms of the loan.
3. Amending the financial ratio reporting requirements of your loan, which are the metrics it uses to ensure that its risk is manageable.

The bank will normally respond in writing, within several days. The outcome will depend on its confidence in your abilities and plan. If you've done your job right, you will get something you can live with. Alternatively, the bank may ask you to take your business elsewhere. This would generally mean forcing you to seek alternative financing, possibly through a loan broker that it suggests, at higher interest rates. This is definitely not what you need.

If all else fails, the bank will call the loan and take legal steps to foreclose. It is its way of minimizing its losses. But it is in nobody's best interests to go this route, if your business can be saved. You don't want it and the bank doesn't need the hassle and the potential adverse publicity. After all, it spends a lot of money to advertise the fact that it is "The banking choice for small business".

In my experience, the essence at this stage is to be creative. Keep talking. Be professional. Enlist professional help in dealing with the bank, if you have not done so already. Don't take no for an answer. Your attitude and persistence will show that you have the resilience needed to work your way through tough situations—just the kind of clear-headed business manager the bank wants to work with.

An example

One of my clients was having trouble in meeting his monthly bank commitment and deathly afraid of tussling with the loan officer at a small, local bank. His school bus company was struggling and the bank threatened to call the loan when payments started to come in late. As a financial consultant, I arranged for Wayne the banker to come out to meet Joe at his place of business.

Wayne knew that Joe never dressed in business duds. In fact, a baseball hat always covered his long hair. A greasy T-shirt and jeans completed his attire.

The meeting was scheduled for the following morning. We had our financial projections on hand. I arrived a few minutes early, but Joe had disappeared. Nobody could find him. I just knew he had run off in fright. As I waited in the office hallway, a rumpled man in casual clothes showed up at the door. Disheveled gray hair emphasized his unkempt appearance. I tried to usher him outside. But his voice sounded familiar. "You must be Ken," he exclaimed. I realized in astonishment that it was Wayne, the loan officer with whom I had spoken by telephone.

It turns out that Wayne wanted to make Joe comfortable, by dressing down. "I'm sorry," I said. "Joe has disappeared. Nobody knows where he is."

At that point, the entrance door flew open. Joe rushed in, resplendent in an ill-fitting bargain-basement polyester suit. A strange and gaudy necktie graced his cheap shirt. A pair of business shoes that looked like they were made of cardboard complemented the effect. "Hi Ken," he said, raising his arm in greeting which, unfortunately, still bore the price ticket, dangling from his sleeve.

He squinted over at Wayne, who stared, open-mouthed, back at him. I almost collapsed, convulsed with laughter. It seems that Joe had been out shopping at the discount store for business duds. Each man had tried to dress the part for the other.

Joe was lucky. We were dealing with an empathetic loans officer in a small, regional bank. We had verbally indicated our position to him and how we wanted it to help us work our way out of it.

The meeting got off to a good start. We presented our proposal and, a few days later, got the revised terms that we had asked for.

I don't want to make light of this story. There's a moral to it, which is to adopt the right attitude and proactive approach. You won't always get a great customer-centered response like Wayne's. But if you are reasonable and try to see the problem from the banker's perspective, chances are, you will get what you're looking for. And in this case Joe's company won. But so did the bank.

A scenario where <u>you</u> are in the driver's seat

The bank is not in the business of assuming your business risk. It intends that the liquidated value of your asset collateral is great enough to cover the loan. But occasionally, the value of a company's assets becomes substantially lower than the loan value. This fills the banker's heart with fear, as he would lose out in a post-judgment foreclosure.

If you personally guaranteed the loan, but your spouse jointly owns the family house, in most states the bank cannot attach this asset. In some states, such as Delaware and Pennsylvania, it cannot attach other jointly owned property. In other words, a judgment holder cannot hold a sheriff sale to dispose of the contents of your family home. The moral of this is not to jointly guarantee business liabilities with your spouse.

Take my client George, as an example. His company manufactures and retails golf related merchandise. He had a substantial bank loan, secured by his house and business assets. His house is jointly owned with his wife and he is the only loan guarantor. Annual revenues sunk much lower than projected. Trade creditors were getting judgments. But we knew that they could not successfully execute and get paid, because the bank had a blanket UCC-lien on all George's personal and corporate assets. In other words, it controlled everything that the judgment holders wanted to seize and sell. From that perspective he was bulletproof, or more specifically, judgment execution proof.

The bank was caught short. George's business asset base had declined. His house and personal assets were untouchable. It was not about to foot a large legal bill to litigate to foreclose on corporate assets worth far less than the value of its claim.

The bank was more than happy to change the terms of the loan to "interest only" for the foreseeable future, to give George's business the chance it needed to put his turnaround plan in place.

If there are no personal guarantees, you are in an even better position. In a situation like George's, with inadequate business collateral to support its claim, you can demand that the banker write down the loan and retire the old one. This takes skill, nerve and professional help, but what outcome could be better than that?

Summary

1. Keep close contact with your bank loan officer at the best of times, but especially when times get tough.
2. Be proactive.
3. Get help from a financial professional to protect your interests, if you don't know how to proceed.

Lesson

Get what you want from your banker through smart, proactive and effective communications.

7

Settle Problem Payables for Cents on the Dollar

It is easy to think that money is the only consideration in a negotiated settlement. It's not, because otherwise bills would always be paid in full, if at all. Your creditor may be short of funds and welcome an immediate discounted settlement—even one at low cents on the dollar. A bird in the hand is worth two in the bush, if they're from a troubled company. It will likely want your future business if you survive, especially if you have been a good customer in the past. Its goods or services may have a high margin and an immediate "haircut" would not hurt too much. Or it may simply fear that your business will fold, as others have done in the past, leaving its account unpaid.

An actual case illustrates the point. My associate and advisor, The Hon. Robert C. O'Hara, a retired and esteemed Delaware Superior Court judge, had just completed an out-of-court settlement to dramatically reduce the large sum claimed by a law firm for legal services. He had pointed out, amongst other things, that the hours billed seemed excessive. And, in any case, our client was unable to pay the entire balance claimed.

No sooner had the ink dried on the settlement agreement than Bob and his wife were enjoying a quiet meal in a restaurant. In the middle of his prime steak he looked up to realize, with some alarm, that the attorney whose fee had been clipped had arrived at the reception desk. Even worse, their eyes locked, upon which the man strode purposefully toward him, emotion flooding his features.

"Oh dear," muttered Bob, "I don't like the look of this." As it turned out, the encounter was pleasant. Extending his arm, the lawyer thanked Bob profusely for resolving the issue, which allowed him to sleep at night. It turns out that the unresolved issue had been eating away at him. He was relieved to see the case finished and done with.

This example confirms that, while money is the central issue and focus of a debt dispute, it is not the only one. Your settlement proposal, whether verbal or written, has to touch on all of the factors that will influence the creditor to make a decision in your company's favor.

Negotiation Basics

The critical elements in any negotiation boil down to three factors

- Time,
- Information, and
- Power

You have to have enough **time** to complete the job. You need as much **information** as you can get about the other side, while providing only that which it needs to know. And you have to retain the **power** needed to maintain control of the process.

Time

The collection industry is under time pressure to collect money. Accounts are assigned to collectors for a finite period, usually no more than six months. If they are unable to collect in that timeframe, they lose control of it. It may go back to the client, get reassigned to others, or passed to a collection attorney.

Collectors will do everything possible to generate urgency. They have to. They tend to work on a commission basis, with monthly quotas to meet. But their agenda is set for their benefit, not yours. You have to be able to address your urgent needs, not theirs.

If a creditor files suit, there is greater urgency to come to a settlement. The court clock starts clicking in the plaintiff's favor. Its attorney intends to make <u>his</u> priority <u>your</u> biggest concern. The time factor becomes crucial, as you have a set number of days to respond. You have to know the ropes in order to either work out a settlement within that limited period, or to file an answer. Depending on size of the claim and the rules of the court, you may need the help of an attorney to counter the claim or to buy more precious negotiating time.

Information

The side with the most information has the best chance of controlling the negotiation. The more we have on the other side's needs and capabilities, the better it is for us. And the more we can provide the other side on our financial and cash position, the less it can argue that we can pay in full. We want to give them the information they need, to permit them to arrive at the decision that we want. But we should not divulge anything that is counter to our own needs.

An example might be a company that plans to litigate to get paid for unpaid merchandise. The creditor and its attorney assume that the endpoint of litigation—a judgment—can be converted to ready cash. If the only information they have before filing suit is an unpaid invoice, then they could be in for a big disappointment. They will likely get nothing if:

- We operate out of leased premises
- The premises are titled to another business entity

- There are no personal encumbrances
- Nothing is owned free and clear, so UCC-1 liens tie up all the company's assets
- State laws do not permit judgment holders to plunder bank accounts.

If so, there's not much point in proceeding, assuming the creditor wants to collect money. If it wants to collect a judgment for a tax write-off, then that's another matter.

A good attorney will generally do his due diligence and get the information he needs before filing suit, in order to advise his client whether or not it will be wasting its money on his services. On the other hand, he might get the go-ahead to bluster and frighten your firm into diverting the cash needed for your firm's payroll and COD supplies into his hands. It does happen to the uninitiated. This brings us to the final element in settlement outcomes...

Power

There are several generally accepted elements of power. You recognize **Situation Power** when a collector calls your company and tries to push you around. Life can be hard for him and he may have little control over other aspects of his life. But he's darned sure that he's in the righteous position of being able to tell you what to do. Recognize this rascal for what he is. He is like the Wizard of Oz. Under close examination his power is nothing but smoke and mirrors.

Mr. Collector threatens to pass the case to an attorney, who has **Punishment Power**, in his ability, as perceived by you, to hurt you in some way, if he does not get his way.

If things don't go well, you can end up before a judge, who has the **Legitimate Power** invested in him by his position, title and black robe.

But before that, you can head off the court date by talking to a business debt management and turnaround specialist, who has **Expertise Power**, by virtue of his knowledge of business dispute resolution.

That person might also be perceived by the creditor or its agent to hold **Reward Power,** in his ability to help, if it cooperates, to get some of the cash that they claim.

And he may get results through **Information Power**, by sharing facts and knowledge and forming a common bond with the individuals on the other side.

At some point, you might ask for advice from an esteemed business leader in your community, respected for the consistent set of values inherent in his **Reverent Power**.

Finally, if all else fails, you can always gravitate to a strong religious leader with **Charismatic Power**, to help you to ask for divine intervention.

The Practicalities of Settling a Debt Problem

In working towards settling a debt dispute when your company is financially distressed and in need of a substantial reduction, you have to consider how the negotiation elements affect the perceptions of the creditor and possibly its collector or attorney. And you have to incorporate these into your discussions and written communications with these people.

My rule no. one in negotiations is to give the other side a good reputation to live up. This stems from the great Dale Carnegie, whose advice appears to have stemmed from the scriptures. Never get into an argument. Form a common bond, if you can, to reach a goal that you can both live with. If someone else gets excited, that's their problem. Let them be that way and stay calm and logical. It helps to stay quiet and let them fume. At some point they'll be willing to talk settlement with you. Put another way, don't wrestle with a pig. The pig loves it and you both get filthy.

Having said that, it is pretty difficult as a business owner or officer to sit still and listen to someone rant and rave, possibly insulting your integrity. But you lose your advantage and your information and reward power, not to mention any reverent power you may possess, if you succumb to a primeval need to retaliate in kind.

Another important rule is to put everything in writing. In all cases where the debt could reach court, it is best to document your settlement proposal. I cannot conceive of just calling someone to make an offer. To me, the reasons are obvious, and are as follows:

- As a literate society, we tend to place more faith in something that's in writing. Your purchase order was likely in writing, as was the invoice. A written settlement offer is a statement of commitment to pay a reduced price in specific, firm terms. It puts it on record.

- If your counterpart is to react negatively to the offer, he can think about it and get back to you once he has calmed down and had time to consider it at his leisure. If you had merely called him, he may well have reacted negatively in front of you, possibly ensuing in a shouting match. It would then be more difficult for him to accept the offer. He would have to "climb down" and possibly lose face by its acceptance.

- A well-written offer is unambiguous and easily understood, unlike a verbal offer. This can be misconstrued, especially when relayed to others, and potentially held against you.

- A written offer can put together an effective story, with complete details on the rationale and the proposed settlement terms, possibly complex and involving a payment schedule.
- A written offer shows that you have invested the time and effort to put it together. In other words, you regard this as serious business.
- A written offer is portable. It can be transmitted and shared by the recipient with all involved in the settlement decision, unembellished with omissions or misperceptions. This differs from the verbal transfer of a telephone call. The message changes each time it is passed to someone else. After a couple of verbal transfers, the actual substance of the offer can be completely misinterpreted.
- A written offer does the creditor's "due diligence" for him. All relevant facts can be laid on the table.
- A written offer makes it easier for the other side to "ink the deal" and signify agreement with your terms.

A settlement is concluded only after you receive an executed agreement from the creditor or its agent, signifying consent on your revised obligation. You should absolutely never rely on a verbal settlement offer. It is always wise to consult an attorney if you need help to see that this is done right, especially if the contested sum is substantial.

Specific Factors Affecting the Process

Negotiations are affected by circumstances surrounding the companies on both sides of the dispute. The ideal situation from your perspective is that the creditor firm is empathetic and responsive to your needs. From your side, the more likely you are to be able to demonstrate that your firm is on the point of going out of business, or that your assets are absolutely bullet-proof, the better.

Let's look at some of these factors, from your each side's perspective.

The Creditor

You are more likely to get a good settlement to meet your goals if the creditor firm can be described as:

- Short of immediate cash. It may be as cash-poor as your own firm.
- Not wanting to compromise doing business with your firm in the future. In other words, it wants you to survive as a continuing loyal customer.
- Having dealt profitably with your firm for a long time.
- Having good personal relations with your firm
- Empathetic and understanding of the reasons for the problem
- Having a high profit margin on the product or service
- Looking at the account from a long -term perspective, involving a flow of revenues over many years.
- Uncomfortable with the initial costs and downside risk of litigation.

On the other hand, the creditor will be less receptive to your offer if it can be described as:

- Having hide-bound, inflexible credit and collection policies

- A large firm, where your firm's future business potential is not crucial
- Not having done much business with your firm in the past
- Having had bad personal relations between key individuals in your firm
- Paying little, if any, attention to your firm's financial position
- Having a low-margin product or service, where non-payment counts highly
- Considering each delinquent payable as a short-term issue to be fixed
- Wanting a judgment at any cost, to "protect its interests"

Your firm—The Debtor

From your firm's perspective, your best protection is to be "bullet-proof" from potential judgments, as earlier described, from both a corporate and personal perspective. Asset protection is the name of the game. This is key, but other factors relating to your company enter into whether or not you will get the negotiated outcome you are looking for.

You will facilitate the best result for your firm if it:

- Has traditionally had good personal relations with the creditor
- Has had a good payment history until now
- Can show that it has been hurt by unforeseen outside circumstances, rather than by bad management (re. empathy and future prospects)
- Can show that there is a real risk of going out of business

- Can demonstrate that the business is bulletproof against judgments.
- Did not attach a personal liability to the account
- Demonstrates that you have worked out a Best Alternative to a Negotiated Settlement, or BATNA. This can otherwise be defined as "walk-away-ability," and may involve the step outlined in Chapter 15 of this book, or other strategies to eliminate the prospect of paying the creditor.

You will face stronger opposition from the creditor if your firm:

- Has encountered trouble or bad-blood between individuals in the creditor firm
- Has entered into a one-off deal, where there has been no history of profitable business
- Has had a poor and troublesome payment history
- Is perceived as deceptive, or is singling out the creditor for unequal treatment
- Has not shown that it has the potential to go out of business
- Can be shown to have attachable assets or, in other words, likely to be able to pay on a judgment
- Has permitted officers to sign personally for the debt, exposing them to risk for unpaid corporate liabilities
- Has no demonstrable BATNA, or walk-away-ability.

These factors are highlighted in Exhibit #2, to illustrate the situations that pose the easiest and toughest settlement scenarios. The most beneficial scenario for the debtor firm is in the top-left section, where positive settlement factors exist on both sides. The least favorable prospect for the debtor firm is on the lower-right quadrant.

In between the extremes, the best prospect for the debtor is on the top right, where its predisposing factors tend to trump the negative characteristics of the creditor. I personally have gotten many of my best settlements in this area.

Using the key elements outlined here, we can analyze two actual settlements in which I have recently been involved. The names have been changed, to protect individual privacy.

Whiz Technologies, Inc.

Whiz Technologies, Inc. got into trouble due to a downturn in its market. The five year-old firm has seven employees. It had got off to a strong but undercapitalized start, in a good niche market. Declining sales, due to a downturn in its particularly fickle market sector had brought the firm to insolvency. It had a negative net worth and could not meet creditor demands.

The landlord was on the point of litigating for overdue rent payments and, more importantly, a major chemical supplier filed suit for almost $300K, including interest and legal fees. The landlord situation was resolved after withholding payments to other creditors, but the large lawsuit promised to put the firm out of business.

The settlement proposal to the creditor's attorney emphasized the fact that the company was in deep financial trouble. Fortunately for us, there were no personal guarantees, so the corporation alone was at risk. But the garage-sale value of the assets was less than $40K, at most.

We proposed $35K as full settlement, this to come from a private loan, personally guaranteed by a company officer. It was turned down flat, the creditor demanding a tough, multi-

Exhibit #2

Key Factors Affecting a Debt Settlement Proposal Outcome

	Positive	Negative
Positive	**Creditor firm (+):** Short of funds - needs cash now Wants future business Dealt with debtor for long time Good relations with debtor firm Understands the debtor firm's hardship High margin product or service Looks at the long-term account value Aware of the downside risk of litigation **Debtor firm (+):** Good relations with creditor Good payment history Hurt by outside or unexpected events Perceived risk of going out of business Shown to be judgment-proof Has BATNA "walk-away-ability" No personal guarantees	**Creditor firm (-):** Hide-bound, inflexible policies Future business not an issue Little experience with debtor firm Bad relations with debtor firm Pays little attention to debtor's position Low margin product or service Wants to "protect its short-term interests" Wants judgment at any cost **Debtor firm (+):** Good relations with creditor Good payment history Hurt by outside or unexpected events Perceived risk of going out of business Shown to be judgment-proof Has BATNA "walk-away-ability" No personal guarantees

	Positive	Negative
	Creditor firm (+): Short of funds - needs cash now Wants future business Dealt with debtor for long time Good relations with debtor firm Understands the debtor firm's hardship High margin product or service Looks at the long-term account value Aware of the downside risk of litigation **Debtor firm (-):** Poor relations with creditor One-off deal or poor payment history Perceived to be deceptive Appears to be able to survive Attachable corporate assets in place Has no BATNA or "walk-away-ability" Attachable personal guarantees in place	**Creditor firm (-):** Hide-bound, inflexible policies Future business not an issue Little experience with debtor firm Bad relations with debtor firm Pays little attention to debtor's position Low margin product or service Wants to "protect its short-term interests" Wants judgment at any cost **Debtor firm (-):** Poor relations with creditor One-off deal or poor payment history Perceived to be deceptive Appears to be able to survive Attachable corporate assets in place Has no BATNA or "walk-away-ability" Attachable personal guarantees in place
Negative		

* BATNA = Best Alternative to a Negotiated Agreement

year payment plan for payment in full. We stayed the course, emphasizing our BATNA. This was to close the company and re-incorporate, in a Dump-Buyback process as outlined in Chapter 15 of this book. We pointed out that we had a range of options open to us, only one of which entitled payment of any kind to the plaintiff. And that $35K was the best we could do.

After weeks of deliberations, during which the plaintiff's attorney granted a continuance, or extra time to settle the matter out of court, we came to a $37.5K settlement as payment in full. The creditor knew that its legal team had done the best it could under the circumstances. It could not squeeze blood out of our stone. This scenario falls within the top-right quadrant in our settlement outcome grid, outlined in Exhibit #2.

Jason Productions, LLC

Jason Productions, LLC, ("JPI") is a small but successful agency involved in promoting classical music productions. It entered into an agreement with a public radio station to produce a show involving a national star. The agency and radio station agreed to share any profits or losses. As it turned out, the event lost $274K, of which half, or $137K was claimed from JPI.

The producer involved in the show left the station shortly after it took place. Current management was unable to sufficiently document the claimed figure to JPI's satisfaction. JPI questioned the veracity of the claim after the station filed suit, which claimed interest, legal fees and other costs, in addition to the $137K.

A personal guarantee was involved in a jointly owned house. There was little prospect, post judgment, of the plaintiff getting paid from this source. JPI had few attachable assets and could, if necessary, close down and re-incorporate.

The radio station was motivated to get paid as much as possible by the end of its financial year. The matter was settled for $47.5K, saving JPI the sum of $89.5K in principal alone.

This deal tends to fall within the bottom-left quadrant of our settlement outcome grid. The creditor's need for ready cash in the short term trumped all other issues. It was not prepared to wait, possibly for a lifetime, for the house to be sold.

The Settlement Proposal

A settlement proposal can take many forms, but it is essential to touch on all the necessary points we have discussed. It has to provide the information necessary for the other side to understand your financial situation and the menu of options that are available to you. It has to be clear that you have a BATNA. And you have to convey in a conciliatory spirit way that this is your best offer. You have to put the information in a form in which the creditor or agent can easily sign off on the deal.

A sample letter proposal is laid out in below. This particular example is designed to settle a case in the hands of an attorney, before it is filed in court. If the suit has already been filed, the proposal's first paragraph can be adjusted accordingly.

A workout, as opposed to the single settlement of an urgent case, involves all the company's debt. This requires additional correspondence, generally starting with a request for time to re-organize and re-group. But the eventual settlement offer has to touch all the bases, as shown in Exhibit #3.

Exhibit #3

Sample Debt Settlement Proposal

YOUR COMPANY LETTERHEAD

Date

C. F. Ikare, Esq.
Wecun Cheatem & Howe
666 Court Square
Philadelphia, PA 19103

Re.: Big Time Equipment Co. vs. My Company, Inc.

Dear Mr. Ikare:

This will acknowledge receipt of your letter of yesterday's date, indicating your intent to collect the sum of (your figure) on behalf of your client in the above captioned dispute. You further mentioned that we have thirty days to reach an amicable agreement, after which you have the authority to file suit.

Our business is currently attempting to resolve a pressing cash flow dilemma and the current obligations that this involves. Management regrets this situation and requests your client's consideration and understanding. Our hope and intent is to be able to settle our firm's many outstanding debt issues amicably, and to be able to stay in business.

Our legal counsel is aware and supportive of our efforts to resolve the company's financial problems by dealing directly with creditors and their agents in this way. If necessary, we will engage his assistance in this matter.

Our firm is in this position because …(add your own bullet points)

We are dealing with the following issues…(add your own bullet points)

We fully understand that we have a certain obligation to your client. Unfortunately, the issues we have described pose a very real threat to our firm's continued existence.

We have identified several options to potentially help us to address these intractable issues. In addition to making settlement proposals that distribute debt payments to the best of our abilities, these include, but are not restricted to (your options):

- *Alternative legal action (Note: don't threaten with the "B" word.)*
- *Closing the company for good*
- *Reincorporating*

UCC-1 liens are in place, covering most of our assets. If we were to distribute to unsecured creditors the fair market value of free-and-clear corporate assets on a pro rata basis, the estimated sum would be equivalent to (your figure as calculated) cents-on-the-dollar.

We desire to seek an amicable resolution in this matter, to permit each party to focus on the more positive and productive aspects of their business. Our current imperative is to dedicate available funds to settlement with your client, rather than to earmark them for legal fees or to the costs involved with any of the other identified options.

Given the situation as described and the alternative options under active consideration, we are under great pressure to make a settlement offer to your client. With great difficulty, we have been able to set aside a sum to potentially resolve the dispute. Many other creditors are pressing for payment and any available funds promise to dry up very quickly. In light of these considerations, we propose the sum of (your figure) as settlement in full.

Payment, via cashier's check, can be delivered to your office within three (3) business days of your affirmative faxed response to my office at (your fax no.)

Thank you in anticipation for your immediate attention to this difficult situation for all concerned.

Very truly yours,

(Your name)
(Your title)

––––––––––––––––––––––––––––––––

Note that the proposal uses, to your advantage, the three key negotiating elements of time, information and power that we have discussed.

You contact the creditor or its agent as early as possible to maximize the **time** available to work out a settlement. If a suit has been served, time is on the creditor's side. You are forced to do the best thing possible to gain momentum. This is to immediately get back to the attorney with a proposal, to use the limited time allowed by the court to your best advantage.

You waste time at this stage at your peril, because inaction can result in a default judgment. And this means that you may be faced later with a uniformed sheriff in your office, clipboard in hand and gun on hip. Not a pretty sight on a Monday morning, especially when it could have been avoided.

You share **information** to meet your own needs. And by freely doing so before being asked and speaking clearly and sympathetically to the debtor's concerns, you tend to form a bond with the other side. By doing so, you are in the minority, setting yourself apart from many in your situation.

The process of sharing gives you credibility and **information power**. And by indicating your company's financial limitations, options and intentions, you show that you possess the **punishment power** to potentially take action counter to the creditor's interests. You also hold **reward power,** to take steps to make payment, if only as a percentage of that claimed.

A Note about Payment Plans

In general, it is easier to negotiate a cash settlement than a discounted payment plan. After all, a cash deal is finished and done with once the settlement funds are in the creditor's bank account. Also, if you negotiate directly for a payment plan at a specific sum per month, the creditor will naturally want the payments to continue until the account is paid in full.

If your company is in trouble, everyone wants a "good-faith" payment schedule if you cannot immediately settle the account in full. The trouble is, there is seldom enough money to do so. Otherwise, you wouldn't be in this position in the first place.

A negotiation strategy to get a payment plan at a substantial savings is to first negotiate a cash settlement. After you get it, go for the "nibble." The decision has been made to accept a specific reduced sum. You just nibble at the other side to accept that figure over time.

Generally, this is negotiated with the creditor's lawyer. He will put "teeth" into the agreement to ensure, to the extent possible, that his client will get paid. After all, your firm has not lived up to its commitments in the past.

You might have the advantage over a professional negotiator in this respect. You just deal with the attorney or collector one time. Those of us who consistently deal with the same collection professionals over a long period are not always able to nibble away at each cash deal in this way. They may come to expect it and dig in their heels after the cash deal has been struck.

As with the reasoning behind the letter proposal we have discussed, the same goes with the payment plan proposal. You have to make it as easy as possible for the other side to accept it. In other words, you have to spell out exactly how the payments are to be made. You have to detail who gets the checks, how they are made out and when and where they are to be delivered. An example is shown in Exhibit #4.

Exhibit #4

Proposed Payment Plan

Big Time Equipment Co. vs. My Company, Inc.

	Date	Payment	Total
2008	January 31	$1,250	$1,250
	February 29	$1,250	$2,500
	March 31	$1,250	$3,750
	April 30	$1,250	$5,000
	May 31	$1,250	$6,250
	June 30	$1,250	$7,500

All payments must be received on or before the dates per the above schedule.

The final payment will constiture settlement in full.

Checks made payable to **Big Time Equipment Co.** are to be delivered to the attention of

C.F. Ikare, Esq.

at the following address:

Wecun Cheatem & Howe
666 Court Square
Philadelphia, PA 19103

I guarantee that this format will give you a much higher chance of success, because you are making it easy for the other side to understand what you propose to do, in precise detail. You are dealing with a creditor who has been waiting for payments.

It may be naturally distrustful, especially if you have been less than forthcoming in the past.

Putting your plan in the detail the creditor needs is a good start. Done properly, you have a good chance of getting a signed settlement agreement. And this is a positive step to help you get back on track.

Summary

1. If your settlement proposal is clear and understandable, with the depth of information contained in the sample letter, you have a good chance of acceptance. Or at least you'll be likely to get a relevant counter-offer. The key is to communicate well and stay the course.

2. Your offer is based on the truth. Unless circumstances change for the better, never deviate far from your proposal in subsequent negotiations. How can you? If you do, it implies that you were bluffing at best and dishonest at worst. You don't need to lose credibility at this stage. And after all, if you have done your number crunching correctly, you know what your firm can and cannot do.

3. You want to do the best you can for your creditors, while permitting your firm to survive. Both sides win. And what could be better than that?

Lesson

President John F. Kennedy said it best—"Never fear to negotiate, but never negotiate out of fear."

8

The Complete Debt Workout
How to avoid bankruptcy and turn your business around

What do you do when there is not enough cash to meet monthly commitments? When payables outstrip receivables and your firm can barely meet payroll, and you get behind with bank, lease and trade commitments? A workout, or composition, as it is sometimes called, is designed to help you stay in business, while minimizing the losses incurred by your creditors. Put yourself in their position. Their worst nightmare is that customers like you will go out of business and pay them nothing.

When companies realize they have run out of options, they tend to either close their doors and walk away, or file for Chapter 7 bankruptcy liquidation. The alternative, Chapter 11 court-appointed workout, would protect from creditors in the meantime and keep the business operating. But it probably involves an up-front payment to a bankruptcy attorney of fifty thousand dollars or more. Business people who have hung on too long often complain that they can't come up with this kind of money. Besides, the vast majority of small firms that file Chapter 11 are quickly forced to liquidate and close down. And it is rare, indeed, for unsecured creditors to get anything of substance from this.

In my experience, most people whose firms are in serious financial trouble don't want to go out of business. They want the opportunity to turn the situation around, or "worked out", to permit them to become solvent, as is the intent of Chapter 11. The trouble is, too many of them either know nothing about it, or receive bad advice and go out of business without any attempt to match their firm's needs with those of their creditors. Everyone strikes out, with the possible exception of the bankruptcy attorney.

The bankruptcy process is cold and methodical, as proscribed by law. There is no need for pleasantries. A voluntary workout is different. Goodwill is important. It emphasizes courtesy and good communications in an environment designed to voluntarily reconcile the needs of creditors with those of your firm. You may need to share appropriate financial information to let others make an enlightened decision.

You have to ask yourself a couple of crucial questions before moving forward and starting a workout. If you could wave a magic wand to eliminate your non-essential unsecured debt, would your cash flow then be strong enough for your business to survive? If not, is there a way to boost revenues quickly at little extra cost, to let you do so?

If you cannot answer these questions positively, then a workout is not going to help. You would need to read the following chapter, on how to dissolve your firm and buy back the assets at garage-sale prices.

The Workout Process

Standard advice is to take stock and evaluate your position, when it becomes obvious that you have to do something to get back on track. This is all very well, but you need breathing space to do so. You and your team need time to be able to step back and review your business plan and take steps to boost net revenues. You cannot do this when you are constantly putting out fires and hiding from creditors.

The first order of the day is to buy time and stop the angry telephone calls. You have to communicate your situation and goals with all unsecured creditors that are not essential to your continued survival. This translates to a period of peace and quiet, to permit future planning. The debt management plan, which is a component of your revised business plan, is designed to highlight and categorize the relative impact of each creditor. Neglect any account at your peril because, left untended, they can quickly litigate in an attempt to grab your assets and potentially close you down.

The debt management plan is your company's road map through the settlement process. A key component of this is your Unsecured Debt Analysis. This identifies the type and urgency of each unsecured liability. Those that are personally secured by you or others are highlighted in bold type, because they may have to be treated with kid gloves. The spreadsheet format that our firm has developed for clients is derived from the accounts payable register and is listed in Exhibit #5.

It is important to identify those contractual obligations that would permit the creditor to close you down at short notice. The terms of loans and leases can often be renegotiated to decrease monthly cash outflow, but these commitments cannot be ignored. Your monthly cash flow planning has to account for these and other costs needed to keep your firm in business and generate revenues.

You or your representative must contact all creditors, in writing, to fully apprise them of the situation. You have to buy time and ask them to work with you. Our firm generally asks for at least 60 days at the outset, to give our client some breathing space and permit it to plan. Each and every unsecured creditor has to know that they are being treated on a fair, pro rata basis, as long as they work with you. They also have to realize that it is worth their while waiting, because your firm is not about to disappear overnight, especially given the plan to turn itself around.

The grace period earned here may have to be extended, given the financial situation. I have personally been involved in workouts where the initial three-month period was extended to more than twelve, until settlement cash was available, after giving creditors regular written updates of the situation faced by the firm.

The available time has to be used effectively, to build a settlement 'war chest,' but more importantly, to make the necessary experience-based changes to your business plan. You need to ensure, to the extent possible, that whatever caused the problem is not going to happen again.

Workout steps depend on some key considerations. How is the debt comprised? Is there unneeded merchandise that can be returned? Are there suits in progress and judgments on file? How long will it take to put together cash for discounted settlements, or payment plans?

A typical workout checklist takes the following form:

1. Project realistic and honest projected gross revenues for the next twelve months.
2. Subtract all monthly fixed costs, together with the costs of essential supplies and services needed by your firm to generate revenues, to arrive at the monthly balance available for non-essential unsecured debt service.
3. Categorize all accounts for workout settlement in the Unsecured Debt Analysis format, per Exhibit #5.
4. Contact those creditors, to inform them of the company's troubles and buy time for payment and

final settlement. A request for 60 days will meet with grumbles, but most should understand, if it is explained properly.

5. Build a 'war-chest' of settlement funds by putting all the identified unsecured debt service funds identified in Step #2 into a separate interest-bearing account.

6. Creatively do everything absolutely possible to find extra cash, as outlined in Chapter 3, by paring costs, selling assets, guerilla marketing or accessing outside capital.

7. Update creditors in writing on a monthly basis on progress being made to generate settlement funds.

8. If necessary, ask for another 30 days.

9. Propose account settlement on an equitable, pro rata basis, as funds become available. Start with those on the upper left-hand quadrant of the Unsecured Debt Analysis spreadsheet.

10. Continue making offers and settlements until the job is complete.

In the final analysis, most creditors will work with you if you are fair and open. But they have to understand that you 'speak softly and carry a big stick.' Knowledge is power. If they threaten litigation, you have to be able to gently remind them that, if push comes to shove, you may be forced to respond by tying them up in court. And this can take years. By that time, who knows if your firm will still be in business? If they want to get paid something on this account and potentially retain a customer in the long term, then this process is sold to them as being in their very best interests. Considering the alternatives, it certainly is.

Exhibit #5

Unsecured Debt Analysis
XYZ Widget Corporation

Ranked by Urgency

Account	Ranked by Balance Owed	Judgment Filed	Suit Filed	Pre-litigation (with attorney)	With Collector	With Creditor
Smith Instruments	$52,889				$52,889	
Utd. Health Care	$37,056					$37,056
Jones Mfg. Corp.	$33,460				$33,460	
Fluid Tech Co.	$25,363		$25,363			
Acer Co.	$24,592					$24,592
James & Hart	$22,134				$22,134	
Austin Insurance	$21,790					$21,790
Canadian Graphic	$21,307			$21,307		
Strobe-Write	$19,460				$19,460	
Centex	$14,921		$14,921			
Harley & Floyd	$14,407					$14,407
XGR Associates	$12,919	$12,919				
Simplex Corp.	$12,192					$12,192
Delta Dental	$11,791				$11,791	
Dell loan	$8,439					$8,439
Totals	$332,720	$12,919	$40,284	$21,307	$139,734	$118,476

The settlements offered creditors reflect, to them, the alternative options available to you. They know that bankruptcy will get them next to nothing. Give them basic financials and an estimate of what that will be. Then offer immediate settlement at several percentage points above that figure. Assure them of your honest commitment to offer the same pro rata settlements to all creditors in their group. Make the offer in good faith, based on reality, and absolutely never make drastic changes to it. Unless your fortunes improve overnight, the first offer would have been wrong. In that event you will have lost credibility. And to many of us, that means everything.

A workout gives creditors the opportunity to make the settlement decisions your firm needs, in their own enlightened best interests. It can be shown to them that they will do better to accept the proposed debt settlements, and retain your firm as a customer—if only on a cash basis for the near future— than to take legal action and possibly force your company out of business. Creditors may be invited to an informal meeting, but this is often not necessary or convenient. Communication by teleconference, fax and e-mail will normally suffice.

From your firm's perspective, a workout provides a number of advantages over Chapter 11 bankruptcy. It holds the promise of a substantially reduced debt load and restructured balance sheet within a much shorter period. Proceedings are private and away from the public scrutiny of the bankruptcy court, which could ruin customer confidence and ultimate profitability.

There is no huge up-front payment, as much of the work can be completed on a contingency basis. A mountain of time-consuming and onerous bankruptcy paperwork is avoided and there is no trustee to look over your shoulder, searching for process illegalities.

A practical example is shown here. Again, the name has been changed to protect individual privacy.

Engineered Test Solutions, Inc.

Engineered Test Solutions, Inc. ("ETSI") is in the business of providing electronic test equipment to major manufacturers of consumer products. Its highly skilled staff produce innovative solutions to the rapidly changing needs of a few, solid manufacturers.

The firm endured a protracted downturn after the events of September 11, 2001. It took years for the market to recover. Just as it did, a major customer filed for bankruptcy, leaving ETSI with $1 million of work in progress and $400K of unsecured debt, for which there was inadequate funding to meet creditor demands.

Approximately forty creditors were involved, of all shapes and sizes. The debt was settled at twenty-four cents on the dollar with funds from a thin new revenue stream. Creditors understood that they could not press too hard. The company's main assets are its expertise and patents and its ability to produce new products.

The deals were struck just before the end of the calendar year, and creditors were relieved to get their books in order prior to the new tax year. Many of them considered, also, that their customer might survive to purchase from them in future, if only on a COD basis for the time being.

This was a workout, involving many creditors, so the settlement motivations of creditors differed. Publicly owned corporations were involved as were small family-owned businesses. But the essential factor driving the deals was that a limited sum was now available and that there was no guarantee that the firm would prevail.

Every creditor but one accepted the deal that was offered, given the risk involved and the timing of the December payout. ETSI's settlement factors, as debtor firm, were paramount, no matter where those of its creditors fell within the grid in Exhibit #2. One creditor refused to deal. It was paid months later, at a fraction more than the others. Given the time value of money, its real return was less.

Conclusion

From your creditors' perspective, the workout holds a prospect of a higher, faster return than in Chapter 11, and certainly more than it would receive if your firm goes under. It takes weeks or months, but not years.

A well-executed process ensures that there is no preferential treatment. Unsecured creditors are offered similar pro rata settlements. The process incorporates clear communication and attention to detail, so few problems can be expected to emerge.

Creditors come to understand that their losses can be minimized and that there is nothing to gain by pushing the company into bankruptcy and closing it down. Considering the alternative, what could be better than that?

Summary

1. A workout in itself will not ensure your future success. But it provides breathing space to analyze what went wrong and establish how to return to profitability.

2. Honest, forthright communications help creditors realize that it is in their enlightened best interest to cooperate, rather than force your firm out of business.

3. If nothing else, your company gets the chance to stay alive, with a healthier balance sheet and better cash flow.

Lesson

Take steps to reconcile your company's needs with those of your creditors—or you'll both lose out.

9

When All Else Fails
How to Create a New Company and Leave your Old Debt Behind

You cannot expect to be able to stay in business unless it generates sufficient income to keep current with creditors. If you get well behind, you can ask them to work with you. Eventually, you may have to work out deals, paying cash or payments at cents on the dollar.

As we have discussed, creditors know that when push comes to shove, it makes better sense to minimize their losses and accept a portion of the sum owed, even if this may have to be paid over time. The alternative would be for them to invest time and money in legal fees and court costs. But they can end up with salt in their wounds with an uncollectable judgment.

The real problem arises when you have tried everything, but just don't have enough cash to propose even these kinds of deals to suppliers.

As captain of a sinking ship in a violent storm you at least have to do everything possible to minimize the consequences. You don't want to go down with it, so you and your shipmates need survival vests and preferably a lifeboat. It would be nice to profit from some salvage later on. And hopefully you will have clear sailing ahead with a new charge, in calm seas.

It is the same with a failing business. You eventually reach a tipping point. It starts to go under, but you don't want to go with it. And you need to do things right to get back on your feet. So what do you do?

There is always bankruptcy, if you want to make your business troubles public and endure a mountain of paperwork, with a trustee looking over your shoulder. The vast majority of small businesses that can afford the high cost of filing for Chapter 11 reorganization will end up in Chapter 7 liquidation anyway. Whereas it's always possible to do what I am about to suggest after liquidating your business assets within bankruptcy, it's not what we're looking for.

The Dump-Buyback

Fortunately, there is hope for a foundering company on stormy seas. It holds the promise of a new venture, after the old one sinks. It comes in the form of a 'dump-buyback.' This is a legal procedure designed to strip your company of its assets and transfer them to a pristine new corporation.

The term derives from the process of dumping, or liquidating, your company. You are then able to buy back the assets at a bargain price, similar to that which others would pay at auction. If you have ever seen valuable business assets auctioned off at a distress sale, you know what salvage value means. Smart people buy needed supplies this way, but that's another story. The cash you pay for these assets is then distributed to your dying company's creditors. You then have the chance to stay in business with a new firm, debt-free, other than the sum that might be borrowed to buy the salvage-valued assets of the old one.

In effect, the company's assets are used to cancel its debt. The lower the estimated distressed value of the assets compared to its debt, the more sense this makes.

If for all practical purposes the assets are understood by creditors to be negligible, they will not be considered worthwhile pursuing. In that case, as so often happens, the debtor company simply closes its doors and says goodbye to its obligations.

It should be pointed out that it is ill advised and dangerous to walk away without giving notice to your creditors. It is of course discourteous and understandably it breeds resentment. This could result in you, as a corporate officer, being sued as an individual. Whether or not the creditor claim had merit, you would be forced to retain legal counsel to file to defend, to avoid the consequences of a default judgment. Win or lose, you can be up against a very expensive outcome. So be careful about walking away without communicating your company's true situation to all creditors.

A dump-buyback makes sense only you if you capitalize on your battle scarred experience to come up with a new and valid business model. You invest funds, possibly borrowed, to buy your old assets at a bargain price, to start a new debt-free company. But it doesn't make sense to do so unless you have learned from the failure of the old venture. If you have not, you may be headed straight back to square one.

You should share your plans with a good business attorney. I personally recommend a collections specialist. These people can be your greatest nightmare when working for your creditors, but your best asset when going to bat for you. They are typically street smart and have seen all manner of illegal tricks and fraudulent asset transfers. You need one on your side to do this correctly and, incidentally, to authoritatively counter moves by creditors' counsel.

The process acknowledges that:

- All corporate assets and liabilities are properly accounted for.

- Assets essentially belong to creditors. You cannot transfer them out of the corporation without paying for their fair market value, as described here.
- Secured creditors have a security interest in specific assets.
- Any personally secured assets have to be left out. Deals have to be struck to handle these separately, because the associated debts will not be left behind.
- Leased property belongs to the lessor and cannot be sold. Permission will likely have to be given for you to transfer a lease to a new corporate entity.

It is understood that you will need to set up a new corporate entity, which will purchase the liquidated assets of the estate of the old company. You then have to complete the following tasks, which are listed in outline form:

1. Communicate your plans, in writing, to all creditors
2. Identify and categorize all assets
   a. Free and clear
   b. Collateralized, as secured debt by either,
   i. The corporation
   ii. Personally secured by individuals
3. Develop a plan to communicate with, and distribute to, proceeds to all creditors—secured and unsecured, including those secured by jointly liable individuals.
4. Hire an appraiser to estimate the liquidation value of these assets.
5. Communicate with secured creditors. Permission

is required for the sale of their assets. It would be fraudulent to do otherwise.

6. Set aside a war chest for asset purchase, or you will need another source of capital to help make the deal.

7. Purchase the assets at a reasonable price, at a slight premium over the figure given to you by the appraiser, to remove any suggestion of a fraudulent conveyance. They can also be bought at auction or through a process known as an ABC, or Assignment for the Benefit of Creditors. You can also liquidate through bankruptcy, but aren't we trying to take a better route—for both your firm and its creditors?

8. Communicate, communicate and communicate.

This process should take weeks, rather than months and, if completed outside of bankruptcy, is private, known only to your firm and its creditors. But it cannot be emphasized enough that communication is the key. Creditors deserve to be fully apprised of what is going on. The least they can expect is courtesy, but silence may lead to suspicion.

It is in your best interests and theirs to let them know that you are engaged in an open process, under the oversight of legal counsel, in the absence of any impropriety. And after all, you may wish to be able to access supplies from them again in the future.

Summary

1. To all intents and purposes, a dump-buyback is invisible to the outside world and your firm is not listed in the newspaper as a filed bankrupt.

2. Your new ship becomes ready to sail, untrammeled by the dark forces of debt that pulled it under.

3. You get a new chance to build that debt-free money machine that you dreamed of in the first place. And what could be better than that?

Lesson

When all else fails, buy your old company back—at a garage sale price.

PART TWO

Build your Turnkey Money Machine

10

Optimism—Don't let it Blind you to Danger

It is unlikely that any successful business is ever started in the absence of an enthusiastic spirit. But this has to be tempered with reason and caution. It can be too easy to get carried away with visions of untrammeled success and an unlimited demand for your goods or services. It is downright dangerous not to consider the downside. Many do so, at their peril.

Even if you don't need a penny of equity or loan capital from elsewhere, your business plan is important. It forces you to think—very carefully—through all the options you can come up with. And the process benefits to you of doing so, and to committing these to writing, are enormous.

Once you have been in business long enough, personal experience of setbacks along the way tends to make you more careful. But when you start out, it is easy to discount the real hazards that you are likely to encounter.

Whatever the stage you are at, it helps to review the reasons why so many businesses fail in this country. If you can understand why other companies are poorly run, you can take steps to ensure that you don't fall into the same traps.

There are as many reasons given for business failure as there are groups and individuals who try to figure this out. My own professional experience relates to entrepreneurs who actually seek help. The very fact that they have done so says a lot about their outlook. They just don't want to think about giving up but positively want to turn things around. And that quality—the ability to handle a crisis—is related to an optimistic spirit and is perhaps the greatest success characteristic of all.

Everyone fails to some extent on their way to success. How many of us could successfully walk or ride a bike at the first try? Walt Disney is reputed to have filed for bankruptcy three times. Donald Trump has had his ups and downs and has twice filed for corporate bankruptcy to protect his business interests. Resilient entrepreneurs take the approach that they have to figuratively roll up their sleeves and do what it takes to get back on track, despite the obstacles.

Stumbling Blocks

Given the need to look at the dark side, the following seven factors are the most common I encounter as the source of the problem, when clients look for help to turn their fortunes around:

1. Inadequate business plan

If you have not worked through your goals and sufficiently established and documented how you're going to get there, you have no road map. In a nutshell—you don't know where you're going. And it becomes obvious to those who are called in to help at a time of trouble.

2. Insufficient access to loan and equity capital

This usually relates to your business plan. In the first couple of years, your business is likely self-financed and any loans—SBA or not—are personally guaranteed. If revenues are inadequate to cover operating costs, you need help.

It is unlikely that you have access to additional equity capital of any kind because, if so, you would have been required to have put together a solid business plan.

3. Inadequate marketing

An inadequate cash flow is a death knell. Lower than expected revenues are generally due to either underestimating the demand for your products or services, or being unable to effectively convince the market that you have the solution that they need. This topic is covered in Chapter 12.

4. Failure to use the services of a coach, business lawyer and CPA

Entrepreneurs in trouble, on their own and without access to a trusted advisor for help, are in a much more vulnerable position than otherwise. A coach, or mentor, can help keep you on target towards meeting the goals you have established. It is now widely recognized in business circles that a coach helps to improve your personal performance and therefore that of your company.

Maintain a strong relationship with a good business attorney. I often deal with entrepreneurs in trouble that have needlessly endangered their livelihoods and exposed personal assets. This could usually have been avoided by consulting with knowledgeable and effective legal counsel.

It goes without saying that you should never sign an important document, which holds you or your corporation financially accountable, without first running it past your attorney. You have to know what the other side can do to you if things don't proceed as planned. And it is too late to question the fine print after problems arise. If someone threatens you, what's your recourse?

As discussed previously, my preference is to deal with business collection attorneys. These people know how to find and seize assets, after a judgment has been awarded. Get one working for you. It is good insurance to anticipate trouble and bulletproof your business. This is discussed in Chapter 13.

Finally, CPA's can provide a wide range of cost-effective services to make your business run more efficiently. My own experience is that clients don't often have the financial tools available to analyze their situation. Clearly, a CPA can effectively set up systems to permit you to immediately find any fact or figure you need. And you have to be able to forecast your cash flow and ask "what if?" questions.

Operating a business without a good accountant on hand can put you at risk. You need the financial tools to do the job and nobody can provide these more effectively than a CPA. If your company gets into trouble, the systems and information made available to you make it easier to prevail.

5. Lack of a systematic management process

As discussed in Chapter 15, a lack of systems equates to chaos. If everyone, including the owner, is fulfilling routine daily tasks in a non-standardized way, then you'll have trouble.

Management decisions in this environment will be based on expedience, rather than properly thought through. This can lead to disaster.

6. Lack of all-round effective communications

Clear communication and attention to detail are super-important in any business. I have found that poor communication in one area is proxy for the same malaise elsewhere. It starts with the owner, or officers, who set the scene.

Creditors can become frustrated at the lack of feedback on the reasons for accounts going unpaid. Sub-par customer service can turn away business. The banker becomes antsy because calls go unanswered. Communication really is the key. If it is a problem, it has to be fixed for the business to improve.

7. Over-dependence on a single individual

If the owner has to be there for the business to survive, you're in trouble. This points to lack of systems. I have seen the outcome of owners falling ill or becoming involved in accidents and being off work for months. It is always a shock. But if there has been no planning to take care of this eventuality, the business is in grave danger.

These reasons for business trouble can generally be avoided. But to do so you have to plan in advance. Enthusiasm is great— as long as it is channeled to consider the many downsides that can impact your business. It can be dangerous at the outset to let it cloud your perceptions of danger, which you are sure to encounter along the way.

Summary:
1. Enthusiasm and the associated positive qualities of crisis-handling ability and resilience can serve you well in your endeavor to build a strong company.
2. The enthusiasm that was instrumental in helping you get your business off the ground, can blind you to potential dangers. And many entrepreneurs fall into this trap, especially at the outset.

Lesson:
Don't let your enthusiasm blind you to the possibility of potential setbacks.

Resource:

Get free and confidential advice from SCORE, 'Counselors to America's Small Business,' which is associated with the US Small Business Administration. Thousands of well-qualified volunteer counselors are standing by, eager to share their wisdom and business savvy with you. Get in touch on-line at SCORE.org.

11

Your Need for a Coach

As an entrepreneur, you're glad not to have a boss. But you are still held to account by your family and employees. And you won't be able to stay in business unless you meet the needs of your customers. It can be lonely at the top, especially if you belong to the Club of Fear.

No matter how independent we think we are, it is of great benefit to have a trusted advisor and coach to help us take the right steps to reach our goals. Sometimes it takes someone else with the experience needed to see the obvious and push us in the right direction. A truly experienced individual is able to identify barriers to our success and suggest tactics and strategies to overcome them.

Many of the best business leaders are coached, as are the top sports stars. Tiger Woods famously stopped using his swing coach for a while. His performance plummeted, after which he realized his mistake. He also uses separate coaches for his business and personal relationships.

The trouble is, most of us are too proud to ask for help. We'd rather struggle through on our own. After all, it was our ideas, enthusiasm and hard work that started the business. We didn't need anyone's help for that. But we can reach a crisis, or a plateau, when our own best efforts seem futile. That's the time when a coach is most useful.

From my perspective and from observing others, I know that an entrepreneur's greatest resource, but biggest handicap, can be the thoughts going through his head. And it is crucially important to keep your head straight, so that you remain resilient and productive. I have seen business people fold their tents, letting down families, employees and customers alike, when all they needed was some coaching from someone who understood their situation and able to guide them through the crisis.

Coaching, in my experience, is a discipline that deals with you, as opposed to specific business tasks, such as marketing or accounting. For example, it may be necessary to tackle your revenue problems by getting marketing advice. But you might very well benefit from a coach's help to pull the whole thing together and dovetail the increased revenues with other plans to grow the business, consistent with your personal goals and capabilities.

Coaching has some similarities in its objectives with Advisory Boards and Mastermind groups.

Advisory Boards

A number of business owners form advisory boards. The idea is to discuss issues on a regular basis and seek direction. Whereas some have had good experience, others have not.

A board is a type of committee. And committees don't always come up with effective solutions. John F. Kennedy once said that, "A committee is twelve men doing the work of one." I would add that, unless there is extremely good chemistry between the different personalities, the advice you receive could be limited.

By definition, the board is in the business of advising. The focus tends to be on your business, rather than on your own personal development as an owner and manager.

The most powerful tool in the development of your

business can be a changed mindset. An advisory board does not necessarily help you in this way. So you are not being coached. Instead, you're being advised what to do. A good coach, on the other hand, can provide the laser-like focus needed to help you to meet your specific goals.

Mastermind Groups

Mastermind groups can be designed to address various business issues, often focusing on marketing. Nothing is more important than increasing revenues and a marketing mastermind group will help you get there.

A good coach may suggest membership in a particular mastermind group to increase your personal and business development. Again, the emphasis is on you, so that you can make the across-the-board adjustments necessary to meet your goals.

If you Google the term "Mastermind Groups," you will be likely to find one aimed at business owners in your geographical area. Another source is Meetup.com, which provides the framework for business people and others to form their own special interest groups. Entrepreneur-related meetups are a popular category, where members are keen to learn and to share their energy and excitement with others. Members meet on a regular basis to discover and discuss cost-effective ways to grow their businesses.

If you cannot find a local mastermind group, you can always start your own. It can be exciting and empowering to learn from others and discuss your own aspirations within a supportive group of like-minded individuals.

Business Coaching Basics

I have asked an associate and renowned coach, author and

business owner, Jerry Wistrom, to describe the benefits offered by a professional business coach. He has a professional career spanning twenty-eight years and is a recognized leader in the business coaching community.

Jerry's extensive background and experience are highlighted on his business website at AllOutCoaching.com. He writes an insightful free daily ezine for business owners, designed to get you thinking. Jerry works with clients all over the U.S. and abroad by telephone, fax and email. He has contributed the remainder of this chapter.

Coaching in Action
by Jerry Wistrom

Tom slouched at his desk, head in his hands. His dejected look mirrored the feelings that were twisting his gut. "I don't know what happened," he said. "I used to feel like a leader and be able to make decisions easily and head on. Now, I feel paralyzed."

Tom owned a landscape management company that had done well in its first few years. It had grown from a couple of guys in a pickup truck to a multi-million dollar business with forty employees. But sales had reached a plateau. He was tired and had lost direction and focus.

After analyzing his situation, we identified a number of reasons for Tom's malaise. We decided on an initial approach to immediately start work on the issue that was causing the most pain—customer service. He was tired of fighting with staff, addressing customer complaints and losing business because of it.

In a short period, Tom was able to restructure the company, built systems and train staff. Those that were unable or unwilling to perform to the new standards were replaced.

A huge weight dropped from his back. Tom was able to address the other issues that we identified and again became able to assume full responsibility for all that happened in his company. He is now a leader—in his own business and also in his industry.

This story is fairly typical. Coaching gives you the ability to access personal help in guiding you towards your goals. It can give you insights in areas in which you had never imagined you needed help. And it can productively keep you on track towards your personal and business goals.

It is important to understand the root problems stopping you from reaching your goals. And to do that, it is also important to recognize the need to change your personal outlook.

We often examine the condition of our business and personal life and look for blame outside ourselves. Of course, when things are going great, we tend to attribute success to our hard work, luck, skill and knowledge. And here lies the key to the entire puzzle. In order to change anything in your life, you have to change yourself.

As you consider that last paragraph, you may be thinking, "Oh no! I'm not going to a shrink. I don't want anyone talking about my childhood!" And you're absolutely right. A coach is not a therapist or psychiatrist. Let's make a quick distinction about that now. A therapist looks to the past to find issues so that they can be identified and brought to light. A coach is entirely concerned with where you are now—and where you want to go.

In order to make the changes needed, you have to take full responsibility for your current situation. When you realize that this is largely based on the actions you have taken, or not, then it's easier to determine the changes necessary to make you and your business successful.

What exactly does a coach do?

Think of a coach as someone to help bring out the best in you. In order to do this, they partner very closely with you. This permits the free exchange of ideas and concepts each way. A coach uses a number of skills and techniques, such as to:

- **Listen**

Coaches are trained to be effective listeners. They listen for consistency and truth. They listen for beliefs that are holding a client back from achieving and they listen for possibilities to explore. This crucial skill permits a good coach to hear things that other people don't pick up on.

- **Question**

A coach forms and asks questions very carefully. The way in which this is done helps you to productively review and explore your current situation and possibilities.

- **Brainstorm**

Many find this to be a main focus of the coaching agreement. You and your coach brainstorm possible solutions to meet your goals. This process is different from that with other people because the entire focus of it is to advance your position. There is no other agenda, as would happen when discussing possibilities with co-workers, family or friends.

- **Strategize**

A bit different from brainstorming where the ideas just build on each other, strategizing is the skill of exploring a number of aspects of a given circumstance. You and your coach will clarify the current situation, establish the intended result and then explore all of the possible strategies to get to that end point. You will then choose and implement one of those strategies for success.

- **Keep you accountable**

Coaches are experts at keeping you accountable to your

plans. Once a course of action has been determined, the coach will determine ways to make sure that you stay on track. This may include emails or phone calls between sessions. The coach holds you to your word. Most business owners have no one to be accountable to, and this service, provided professionally, can be of great value to you.

- **Help you make the right decisions**

Professional coaches are trained to help you find your own solution and make the best decisions possible. The coach will often help you see the ramifications of each possible solution and look for a "best fit" to the specific problem. This solution will often take into account a number of factors and variables including:

- Is this a short term or long term solution?
- Does it align with your values and beliefs?
- Does this solution fix the underlying problem, or just the symptom?
- What are the deciding factors in finding the right solution?

What should you expect from a Professional Coach?

- **Confidentiality**

Most coaches will sign a full confidentiality agreement with you, insuring that none of your business plans or ideas will be discussed outside of your relationship. Most coaches will not even name their clients, based on this level of confidentiality.

- **Partnership**

Expect your coach to be like a partner to you, with only your agenda and success in mind. No professional coach will ever tell you what to do. Every commitment to action is reached as an agreement, not an order.

- **Safety**

This may sound a bit strange, but you should expect to be completely safe with a coach. They are trained to be accepting of everything they hear and are ready to help their clients move forward from there. You will not be judged or criticized. You can completely be yourself in this relationship.

- **Honesty**

Your coach will be brutally honest with you. Whatever needs to be said, will be said. There is no holding back. Expect that honesty to come with a lot of compassion when needed, but the honesty will always be there.

- **Focus on "You"**

You can expect that every minute your coach spends with you will be focused directly on you and your learning and development.

- **Personal Growth**

Working with a coach is probably the quickest way to grow yourself, either personally or professionally. Although the coach is helping you to tackle business problems and issues, you're the one who really gets the growth. Expect to become a better business owner, manager and person.

What will a Professional Coach expect from you?

A number of expectations will be made, each meant to optimize your coaching time and maximize your progress. In no particular order, every coach will expect:

- **Honesty**

In order to help you explore your current circumstances and determine the best path to follow, you have to be honest with your coach—about everything. You may never have had the opportunity to be as open with another professional. But in this relationship you'll get the most out of being completely straightforward in everything you discuss.

This relationship is based on partnership, and a full partnership is not possible without complete candor. Don't sugarcoat facts or hold back on your strengths and weaknesses. Tell the truth and it will help in the process of meeting your goals.

- **An Open Mind**

One of the reasons you're hiring a coach is to go places that you haven't been before. It is essential that you remain open to the ideas and processes that you and your coach go through. Closing down your options will only hurt you and your progress.

- **Progress**

Your coach will work with you to set commitments as to what you'll work on between your sessions. Make sure that you do what you have agreed to. Your success will depend on your following through as planned.

- **Responsibility**

Your coach is going to make it very clear that you are responsible for your own results. The work here is not the coach's—it is yours. You have to take responsibility for your work and your business.

How do you to hire a Coach?

At this point, the coaching world is split into two camps—those who are trained and accredited and those who are not. The coaching profession has become mainstream and many people now call themselves coaches. Psychologists are marketing themselves as such. Consultants are hanging up the "coaching" shingle. People who have been recently displaced from corporate America have business cards with the title "Coach." Beware!

A number of organizations certify coaches. The ICF, or International Coach Federation, is becoming the standard for the profession. When hiring a coach, look for someone who is a member in good standing, and has the certification of MCC, PCC or ACC. These three levels of certification let you know that you're working with a certified professional coach.

Check the ICF website to check coach credentials at Coachfederation.org/ICF.

Use the same link to search for accredited coaches, based on certification, geography, gender and other requirements that you specify.

Interviewing a Coach

Before you hire a coach, you should have a combined interview and complimentary session. Most professional coaches will coach you for thirty to forty minutes to help determine if there is a fit for both you and the coach. My suggestion is that you interview two or more coaches before deciding.

As you go through the session, notice how well the two of you communicate. Is this person easy to talk to, or is it a strain? Also notice how you feel through the session. Are you at ease, or uneasy? Do you feel comfortable, or on edge? Is the coach's style a fit for you?

Most coaches that you interview will gladly recommend other coaches for you to talk to, before you make your decision. Feel free to ask the coach for their recommendations based on what you're looking for.

Evaluate the Contract

Evaluate a coach's contract the way that you would that of

any other professional. Is there a commitment for length of time? Is there a clear-cut way to end the relationship? Is there a guarantee involved? Is there a charge for missed sessions, or extra time?

How to Evaluate the Effectiveness of the Relationship

You are looking for progress towards specific goals. And this is the only way to evaluate effectiveness of the work that you do with your coach. If you can answer with a resounding "yes," then you're in a great relationship. If not, you have to bring this up with your coach and determine what is lacking.

Summary

1. A coach differs from other professionals in that the focus is on you and your goals, rather than a specific task or business service. This brings out the best in you.

2. The best business leaders use coaches to help maintain focus and succeed in their personal and business life. You can benefit in the same way.

Lesson

Get professional help to maintain focus and achieve your personal and business goals.

12

Seven Steps to Effective Marketing

Chances are, if you've had cash flow trouble, your marketing has been at fault. Not always, though. I've worked with businesses that had been put on the ropes after major customers filed bankruptcy, or just disappeared into the night.

This can be especially traumatic when you have a substantial amount of work in progress, dedicated to that firm. But many financial problems derive from ineffective marketing. Perhaps the product or service mix you provide is inadequate, or you just don't have enough customers, or you're not selling enough. Whatever reason, the cause for inadequate revenues has to be identified and dealt with.

Every great company is market focused. This might seem obvious, but you just can't succeed without knowing what your market actually wants. I had experience with this when an environmental equipment manufacturer built a beautiful piece of equipment at significant cost, to remove toxic chemicals from groundwater and wastewater. The engineers involved were tremendously proud of their achievement. They were in love with their own product, as was the technically oriented president. It worked beautifully and was a handsome, crowd-pulling exhibit at industry trade shows.

The trouble was, the firm had inadequately assessed its market. In fact, it was so convinced of its superior technology that there had been no test marketing. If truth be told, the company was production-driven and ignored competing technologies which, while less elegant, were cheaper and just as effective. Nevertheless, staff was hired to sell this equipment across North America. The outcome was unfortunate—not one single unit was sold. This was the straw that broke the camel's back. The company was forced out of business.

I have seen astonishing examples of market-driven producers in niche areas who well exceed the incomes of others in the same business. An immigrant greenhouse grower in Ontario, Canada, for example, constantly develops and produces new houseplant varieties for the North American market.

These plants fetch high prices in a traditionally low-margin, commodity-based business. The entrepreneurial grower has no interest in being a commodity price-taker. Instead, he takes the time to research his market and produce what the consumer is looking for before his competitors catch on. Market research helps the business stay well ahead of the pack and generate high margins in doing so.

For some of us, even after we do everything it takes to understand our market and customers, we are reluctant to effectively promote our businesses. Especially with smaller firms, a psychological barrier can be involved. Many of us were raised not to "toot our own horns." If so, we have to overcome a natural reluctance to let everyone know that we really do provide the best solution to meet their needs. After all, if we don't do it, who will?

Here are seven crucial marketing concepts to bear in mind if you are to take your business to the next level:

1. Understand the importance of marketing to your business.

Every great business stands on three legs. Yours has to offer good products or services. It must deliver a great experience for its customers. And it needs to market itself effectively, so that people know about it. Unless all three legs are in place, the business will fail.

I know from experience that many companies realize the crucial importance of marketing only after getting into financial trouble. Fortunately, when times are tough, getting on the right track is not always as difficult as it might seem. But it takes applied knowledge to get there.

If you still find it difficult to think like a marketer, or your firm doesn't have the skill set to effectively market, hire a professional. Get someone to use their expertise to help you to come up with an effective strategy, based on your target market. What remarkable solutions do you have to offer these people, or businesses? Who are they? Your main goal has to include them in your prospect database. Then you have to focus your marketing efforts them.

2. Be clear about <u>who</u> you want to sell to.

There are riches in niches. Many people think much too broadly. Focus on being the best solution to meet client needs in a specific area, or areas.

Famous bank robber, Willie Sutton, knew how to focus. Asked why he robbed banks, he is famously said to have answered, "Because that's where the money is." He wasn't about to waste his time and energy looking for money in the wrong places.

It's important to know how many of your specific customers are looking for your products or services. This can pose a real challenge, but if you can sell online, you can do this with pinpoint accuracy. Wordtracker.com lets you figure out current consumer demand. And it also gives you an idea of the extent to which your competition is responding to it.

Wordtracker lets you do a full keyword analysis of the terms people are using when searching online for information. This is based on all searches carried out on MetaCrawler.com, DogPile.com and the Overture (Yahoo) Pay per Click network. You can plug in as many single keywords, or keyword phrases, that you think people will likely be using.

Wordtracker gives you the frequency of each search term. It also provides a KEI, or Keyword Effectiveness Index value, to let you estimate your competition represented by their use of that search keyword or phrase. This calculation of likely competitiveness compares the number of times the keyword phrase was entered in twenty-four hours with the number of matches found for it on potential competitors' websites. The higher the KEI number, the less competition you have. A good KEI would be 100 or more, while an excellent one is considered to be over 400.

In a nutshell, Wordtracker is the tool to use to find and exploit currently underserved niche markets. And it will tell you whether or not the words and phrases used in your marketing materials are those that people are actually using when looking for your goods or services.

3. Concentrate your marketing budget on direct response.

Direct response marketing focuses your company's scarce resources so that each dollar's response rate can be precisely measured. This form of marketing uses many types of media, including the Internet, direct mail, postcard decks, newsletters and catalogs. The key is to be able to track feedback and establish accountability for the results that you get.

You want the intended recipient to read your message and then take action to contact you or, better yet, give you the order.

It is of crucial importance to keep excellent records and test response rates of variants to a known standard ad., so that you can maximize your results.

Direct Response ads incorporate a strong, bold headline with an effective call to action. They provide a clear outline of benefits and incorporate an offer for prospects to respond to.

Direct response marketing is sometimes confused with institutional advertising, which has no call to action and is intended to build brand identity, awareness and familiarity.

This is a specific area in which you can benefit from the expertise of a professional, to help you on your way. At the very least, you have to read as much as you can on the subject. Take action now to throw out ineffective marketing materials and develop smart, cost-effective ads to win new business.

4. Capitalize on the three-step business development formula

Your business development process is limited to three activities:

1. Increasing the number of customers
2. Increasing the frequency of sales per customer in a given period, and
3. Increasing the dollar value of each transaction.

Your new customers take time, money and effort to acquire. Despite your best efforts, not all of them will stay with you. Your goal is to convert them from one-time 'transactional' buyers to long-term 'relationship' buyers and capitalize on their lifetime customer value. It's not smart to sell one item, then to completely ignore their existence.

You can only communicate with your customers if you have taken the time to build a list. And this can become your most precious business asset. If your business burns down and you still have your list, you have a much better chance of recovery. Clearly, you have to take the right steps to capture customer names, telephone numbers and addresses, including email.

Once you are past the startup phase, the real money lies in increasing your back-end business. This comes from a loyal group of relationship buyers. The key is to intensify both the frequency and magnitude of sales to this group and to have them refer others to your business. And you can only achieve this by providing exceptional value.

If you run into a slow period and need extra cash flow, high margin sales to your current customer base can pull you out of hot water. As a simple example, if you operate a restaurant, you can immediately bring in business by sending out a direct-response email to your "preferred guest" list with a time-sensitive special offer.

5. Use free publicity

One of the best ways to let people find out about your business is to publish an article or press release, or get on radio or T.V. Free publicity beats having to pay for it. An interesting story can generate a lot of interest and credibility.

Local news media are always looking for interesting stories. Tell them about yourself, as company founder or owner. What does it take to run a successful business? How have you overcome adversity? What have you learned? With a little thought, you can get a lot of exposure and credibility with minimal expense.

Press releases have a longer reach. If you have something of interest to tell, such as a new way of doing something or a new product, send a press release to selected publications. Ereleases.com is one source to help you to write and distribute press releases.

Trade magazines are always looking for an angle on a story.

Contact the editor with a story idea—perhaps an innovative way to handle a common problem, for which your firm has the answer.

If you have problem putting your article together, imagine that you were talking to a friend about the subject. Tape-record your imaginary discussion. At the end of the piece, add your name, email and company.

Submit articles to as many online magazines as possible. This is a very smart way to promote your business. It can lead to contacts and new business that you had never dreamed of.

6. Use multiple marketing methods

Government regulation and technological advances continue to force change in marketing strategies. Telemarketing is now constrained by "do not call" lists. Fax broadcasting has been restricted. Who knows what changes may impact Internet marketing?

There is real danger in depending on a single source of business leads. A smart company enhances its resilience by using a wide variety of marketing methods. If any one approach becomes less effective, others can compensate the impact.

7. Associate with like-minded people who are also looking for solutions.

As a fully-fledged member of the Club of Fear, you need to be able to develop and implement the marketing solutions you are looking for. The whole business of marketing is so crucial to your company's success that you have to constantly stay abreast of developments.

Earl Nightingale once said that anyone could become an expert in their chosen field if they studied for an hour a day, every day, for five years. You might not be able to become an immediate marketing authority in the short term, but you do need to find out as much as you can on the subject.

One of the keys to help you get started is to share your issues and ideas with a group of like-minded entrepreneurs. Join a marketing based mastermind group, as outlined in Chapter 11. Get involved in local business groups and organizations. Give other business people the opportunity to see what you do and have to sell—and how this can benefit them.

A note concerning Sales

Are your sales people driving away the leads that your marketing efforts provide? Dale Carnegie said that you will sell far more by becoming interested in your customers than by them becoming interested in you. You will be much more successful in converting your leads into paying customers if you do so.

Your sales people will demonstrate their interest in your customers' satisfaction by asking open-ended questions. This will help meet their goals, while improving your closing ratio and developing a list of loyal, satisfied customers.

I saw this process in action when recently attending a fine craft and furniture show with my wife. This was a big event in Baltimore, for which the exhibitors had clearly spent heavily to bring in merchandise from all over the country. We were looking for a unique table for our home.

After talking to a number of vendors, only one representative took the time to ask specific questions about what we really wanted and how much we were prepared to spend. Once he understood what we were looking for, he showed it to us. The others we had visited had either simply focused on the merits of their furniture, or worse, sat at the back of their booths, asking visitors to sign up for a mailing list.

He produced a purchase order, which we filled out and signed on the spot, paying by credit card. We are now confirmed, satisfied customers. The representative turned out to be the owner of the small manufacturing company that bore his name. (ScottGrove.com). He knew how much it had cost him to get there from a day's drive away, and to set up at the Show.

Scott wasn't going to let this sales opportunity slip away. He was the only exhibitor to ask us anything about ourselves—and then to tailor his response accordingly. We feel like we know him. He deserved our business. We recognize that and intend to buy more of his furniture.

Summary

1. Marketing is a hugely important function on which every successful company is based.

2. Invest your money in direct marketing in order to measure response and maximize revenues.

3. The most cost-effective way to develop additional revenues is to increase the level of business conducted with your current base of satisfied customers.

4. You don't always see the obvious, or make the necessary connections, to immediately understand what needs to be done. Seek help from professionals in this field and associate with like-minded people.

5. Take effective steps to convert your hard-won marketing leads to sales.

Lesson

Take the steps necessary to drive your company to the marketing-based success it deserves to be.

13

Build a Resilient, Bulletproof Company

The idea of a bulletproof company is that, come hell or high water, nobody can take it away from you. It is kept within a corporate shell and your business arrangements are made in such a way that creditors are unlikely to be able to touch it. And creditors aside, we live in a litigious society where someone might be angry, wealthy or nutty enough to pay an attorney to try.

Think of the worst possible setup, where your business is operated as a sole proprietorship or partnership. Few partnerships work well, in my experience, because only one person can be the "boss". But that's beside the point. With an unincorporated company you are personally liable for each and every business debt. Your house is on the line and possibly your marriage, in the likely event that you run into problems.

Things can get worse. What if the business premises or other real estate is in your own name? If your business fails, you can lose every last cent and still be forced into personal bankruptcy, possibly followed by the divorce court.

1. Incorporate or form a Limited Liability Company (LLC)—an absolute must

Your first priority has to be to build a corporate shield. You should do it at the outset. You can incorporate, or form an LLC, on-line for a few hundred dollars. In fact, even if you are up and running as a sole proprietorship or partnership when you get into financial difficulty, you should still incorporate, under your current "doing business as" name.

Legally, any debt that was incurred prior to the incorporation date is personally liable. You are likely to have filled out a credit application with each supplier of goods or services. If you have since incorporated, chances are that not all of your creditors will check to find out your original status.

2. Keep your corporation asset-poor

If you have few assets, creditors have little to attach. Your company, as the operating corporation, absolutely should not own real estate. Don't give a judgment holder the opportunity to attach it, or any other valuable asset, such as essential equipment.

Sad to say, all too many businesses lose their premises when they fail, so they lose twice—the business and the real estate. At best, as a business debt manager, I can often negotiate reductions in the liens prior to sale, to let the owner walk away with something. This shouldn't have to happen.

The key is to run a lean, mean asset-poor machine. When times are good, it can be hard to foresee clouds on the horizon. But if you run into trouble, your creditors' attorneys will soon discover your asset base.

Your first priority is to protect your business. Creditors' needs are important and must be respected. But you can't help them if your means of generating income and future business is taken from you.

3. Use Friendly Liens to armor your company against creditors

A lien is a form of secured instrument, placed on your business property to protect a lender or lessor. Known in this country as a UCC-1, it gets its name from the Universal Commercial Code, or UCC, adopted in the 1930's by virtually all US States. These liens are filed in the office of the Secretary of State in the specific state to which it applies. This information is made available to anyone for a fee, either directly or indirectly through private agencies, such as Lexis-Nexis and Dun & Bradstreet.

The mortgage on your house will be secured in this way. The first-mortgage lender's interests hold a priority over subsequent claims, such as those of second-mortgage holders, who may place liens on the same property at a later date. Another form of lien is a judicial lien, put in place subsequent to legal action. And then there is the dreaded tax lien.

A friendly lien serves the same purpose as the unfriendly variety in that it is a claim on property, placed by a creditor. Also filed as a UCC-1, in this case you want it to be there. It is placed specifically with the intent to protect your business assets. At the same time, it represents a genuine financial obligation by your corporation to the individual or business entity that placed the lien.

The lien can be placed by:
- You, representing loan capital and unpaid wages.
- A friend or relative, who is owed for work done or loans provided.
- A preferred trade debtor, with whom you have a good working relationship and who will agree to a mutual-protection strategy

It is highly recommended that you retain an attorney to draw up the promissory note, which corroborates the claim, and then file the UCC-1. This will ensure that the task is completed properly. This is important, because you don't want to expose your corporate assets to a potential judgment holder.

4. Spread your risk—through separate corporations

If you have several ventures, they're not all likely to succeed. Don't risk the lot by operating under one corporate umbrella.

A small chain of restaurants I dealt with, which was incorporated as one entity. Major problems at one of the locations almost put the entire firm out of business. The company had a narrow escape, from which the owner emerged a lot wiser.

Each restaurant now operates as an independent corporate unit. If necessary in future, a sick branch can be chopped off, leaving the rest of the business to survive.

5. Protect your most precious corporate asset—your customer list

The more established your business becomes, the more crucial to your survival is your customer list. If you are thrown out in the street tomorrow, you are in much better shape if you still have your customer list. After all, your easiest and most frequent sales are made to established, satisfied customers.

Your customer list has real market value. It gives your business resilience. If you run into trouble and want to close down, it can be sold to others. Or you can transfer it, for use in another business.

When your customer list includes established, long-term customer contracts, you can lose them in bankruptcy. Given that these contracts represent a virtually guaranteed stream of future income, they have a market value and can be sold. A Philadelphia-area bottled water company ran into this problem. It was unexpectedly unable to keep its customer list after filing bankruptcy, which it had intended to use to sell competing bottle-less coolers—using municipally fed filtered water. This made it much more difficult to start afresh.

If you want to keep control of your list, but believe that

your business is headed for bankruptcy, make sure to avoid long-term contracts. But do everything possible to hang on to your customer list because, contracts or not, it can represent your ticket to new business success.

Personal asset protection

It goes without saying that your corporation or LLC protects your personal assets. You absolutely do not want to lose everything you own in a business venture that goes sour. Don't make yourself personally liable.

You have to protect your personal assets by doing everything possible not to sign personal guarantees. At least, keep them to an absolute minimum. Your banker will want one, unless there is enough corporate equity to secure the debt. But your business's corporate status provides protection from personal liability. And it doesn't make sense to throw this away. You have to have "walk-away ability" whenever you are asked to fill out a personal credit statement for goods or services. Either have the supplier accept your business without it, or take steps to access goods and services elsewhere.

As an entrepreneur, you have to have some Dr. Jeckyl and Mr. Hyde in you. Whereas you don't want to sign personally, you have to try to get personal guarantees from your clients or customers. Those signed by both spouses, when they possess jointly owned property, are especially effective.

I often deal with business people who are shocked to have been sued personally for non-payment of goods or services received by their firms on credit. Typically, they mistakenly thought they were signing an agreement as a corporate officer, rather than a personal guarantor. This problem can be avoided if you routinely use a "signature block." This clarifies that the signatory—you—is acting as representative of your corporation, or LLC.

The block can be purchased on-line and through office supply stores and looks like this:

ABC, Inc.

By: _____

John Henry, President

A final mention should be given to disability insurance. What will happen to your business if you have an accident and are incapacitated, or fall ill, for a few months? This will depend on the size of the company and whether or not you have systems and people in place to shoulder the load. In any event, talk to your insurance agent if you're not covered. This can provide significant protection and could mean the difference between your business's survival or disaster.

Summary

These strategies serve to form your main line of business and personal defense in times of trouble:

1. Incorporate, or form an LLC
2. Keep your business asset-poor, so there's nothing to attach
3. Use friendly liens to protect your assets
4. Spread your risk—through separate corporate entities
5. Protect your most precious corporate asset—your customer list
6. Act like Jeckyl and Hyde—and get disability coverage—to protect personal assets and your livelihood.

Essentially, these steps will go far to ensure that you

maintain control of your destiny, despite the potential actions of hostile creditors.

Lesson

Take the initiative and build a bulletproof company, impervious to hostile creditors.

14

Build your Business Credit and get rid of Personal Guarantees

How would you like to have lines of credit for your business, completely unsecured and devoid of personal guarantees? If this interests you, you are not alone. But if you take positive steps to do something about it, you will be in a small minority.

Why is this? Probably because it is too easy to use your own credit, and that of friends and family, in the optimistic and mistaken assumption that your business will never get into trouble. As well, the process by which you are able to build your business credit is not universally known or discussed.

Think of it this way. Your personal credit is tied to your social security number. It is monitored through three major credit reporting agencies, these being Equifax, Experian and TransUnion. Your corporate credit, on the other hand, is tied to the unique identity that is your company.

Business Credit Basics

Credit can be established solely on your company's behalf, be it a corporation or LLC. Dun & Bradstreet, or D&B, forms the gold standard for business credit reporting and originally developed the concept. Equifax Business and Experian Business are more recent entrants to this field.

An unsecured business line of credit can make a significant amount of short-term cash, supplies or services available to your company when you need it. As with your personal credit cards, it is not asset-based, so collateral is not required. Good business credit can also help access better financing rates and terms for a wide variety of goods and services, including leases and insurance.

It can be very difficult to get purely business credit before your company has been operating for a couple of years. The few exceptions prove the rule. If your bank is familiar with you and you have excellent personal credit, you might be able to get what you want from that particular institution.

It takes time to build up business credit, just as it does the personal variety. Imagine trying to get a house mortgage, or a new vehicle, with no history in your credit report. The lender needs to predict whether its payments will be kept on track, but would have nothing to go on. The same thing applies to businesses. Your company won't get anything unless it has been around long enough and can show that it is sufficiently well managed to be an acceptable risk.

You have to build comprehensive credit files and ensure that your company's bills are paid on time. This includes bank loans, leases, trade suppliers and utilities. The business credit reporting agencies report your firm's liabilities, including any liens and judgments, and its bill-paying experience.

Keeping current with your accounts payable is a positive indicator of a good lending risk. D&B originated its PAYDEX score for this purpose. Most companies will not approve credit without reference to it.

D&B's competitors, Equifax and Experian, have their own way of measuring bill payment timeliness. It's called Days Beyond Terms, or DBT, and is graphed over time, to show trends. Unlike PAYDEX, the higher the number, the worse the perceived credit risk.

These payment scores reflect only the experience of vendors

that report to a particular agency. Any potential credit supplier can pull a D&B or competing report to determine whether or not it wants to do business with your firm. The higher the PAYDEX score, the better the risk, on a scale from zero to 100. (Exhibit #6)

Exhibit #6

PAYDEX Score Ratings

PAYDEX Score	Reported Payment Experiences
100	30 days sooner than terms
90	20 days sooner
80	ON TERMS
70	15 days beyond terms
60	22 days
50	30 days
40	60 days
30	90 days
20	120 days
0-19	Over 120 days

A PAYDEX score of 80 can be considered equivalent to having an excellent personal (FICO) credit score of 800.

There is no universally understood business credit score, shared by all agencies, similar to the FICO score used in consumer credit. Of many types of indices, the US Commercial Credit Score (Exhibit # 7) is based on D&B data only. It predicts the likelihood of a firm becoming delinquent with its payables (ninety-days late, or more) within the next twelve months. The figures shown here highlight the high level of risk faced by business owners—either in getting paid by creditors or being able to stay in business.

Exhibit #7

U.S. Commercial Credit Score Index

Commercial Credit Score	Credit Score Percentile	Credit Store Class	Incidence of Delinquency
536-670	91-100	1	2.5%
493-535	71-90	2	4.8%
423-492	31-70	3	12.9%
376-422	11-30	4	24.2%
101-375	1-10	5	58.8%

D&B currently reports the Incidence of Delinquent Payment (ninety days or more overdue) for all firms in the United States to be 17.3%. The Incidences of Delinquency listed for each range shows the percentage of firms that paid in a delinquent manner over the past year.

Each of the three agencies compute their own ratings and critical indices to estimate financial strength and stability. Lenders typically use computer analysis to dig into underlying data to assess potential funding eligibility. Since loan decisions less than $100,000 tend to be automated in this way, your business credit file will determine the amount and terms of a business loan. Trade suppliers, on the other hand, tend to place more reliance on PAYDEX and DBT scores.

Building your Personal Credit

A strong personal credit score is important because, even if you wean yourself off having to use your own credit, it is still interrelated with the business. As a small business owner you may still be asked to provide personal information, even though you are not signing personally for credit. It is assumed to reflect personal responsibility. For example, Equifax produces a blended Small Business Credit Risk Score. D&B, on the other hand, restricts itself to purely business data.

The Fair Credit Reporting Act protects your personal credit report data. In short, your personal credit information can be accessed only by those to whom:

- You are personally obligated in the credit obligation, or
- You have provided written instructions permitting access to your consumer credit file.

The information on each of your credit reports is boiled down to a FICO score, developed by the Fair Isaac Corporation. This number ranges from 300 to 850. Two percent of consumers have scores less than 500. Thirteen percent have scores over 800. Fifty-eight percent have a score in excess of 700. You will at least want to be in this range to be considered a good credit risk.

The three credit reporting agencies each produce their own FICO score, so you have three scores. These will likely differ from each other by a few points, because of differences in the data in each file. Just to be different, Equifax's score is called Beacon, while TransUnion uses the term Empirica.

The FICO score breaks down into five basic categories, as shown in Exhibit #8.

Exhibit #8

FICO Score Assessment Breakdown

Payment history	35%
Amounts owed	30%
Length of credit history	15%
New Credit	10%
Types of credit in use	10%

The largest single category is "payment history". "Amounts owed" is almost as important, and is a measure of whether or not a person is overextended. These are factors that you can immediately work on to make a significant impact.

A proven strategy to increase your score is based on these FICO realities. It recognizes that maxxed-out credit will lower your score, but that regular repayment of significant sums of borrowed money, on time, has a positive impact. So it involves the following steps:

- Borrow as much money from your each of your credit card accounts as is possible, <u>without</u> reaching your actual credit limit.
- Set the money aside in a bank account.
- When each monthly payment is due, withdraw the funds required from your bank account and pay the borrowed balance in full.
- Repeat the process each billing period.

Do this with all your credit card accounts. You will positively impact the 65% of the FICO score determined by payment history and amounts owed. This will quickly build a favorable payment history and show that you borrow well within your limits. This will result in offers of increased credit limits and your score will soar.

Apart from other obvious advantages, an improved FICO score can give business lenders and suppliers confidence in your capabilities, even when your personal guarantee is not required.

Building your Business Credit

So how do you set things up so that your company has access to lines of credit, linked only to your business checking account? Fortunately, you don't have to own a multinational corporation. On the other hand, it takes time and effort on your part to get the job done.

The initial task is to establish a comprehensive business credit file, or profile, with each of the three business credit bureaus. The credit reporting business is highly competitive and each agency handles this process differently. Your business should have a bank loan, three business credit cards and six lines of credit from suppliers. The basic information you should have on hand, before contacting each agency, is highlighted in Exhibit #9.

Exhibit #9

Business Credit Bureau File
Initial Setup Checklist

Heading
Full corporate/business name:
Doing business as (otherwise known as D/B/A):
Legal structure (Corporation or LLC)
License type; Number; Locality:
Physical address:
Mailing address:
Employee total:
Year Company started:

Executive listing
Chief Executive and title
   % Stock owned
   Work experience in previous five years
   Education
Other officer(s)
   % Stock owned
   Work experience in previous five years
   Education

Operations
Line of business
SIC code
Building rented, lease or owned?
Square footage
Type of building

Trade reference
Add all trade suppliers that provide credit:
   Company name
   City and State
   D&B DUNS no.
   Telephone no.
   Fax no.
   Account no.

You can quickly establish a good business credit rating with all-important D&B by using its D&B's CreditBuilder Plus process. Experian and Equifax do not currently offer this type of service.

You can access D&B's online expedited service at Smallbusiness.dnb.com, or by calling the agency at 800-234-3867. This involves D&B specialist staff, who commit to building an effective business credit file as quickly as possible. You are initially requested to provide comprehensive corporate information, including up to six trade references.

D&B will assign your firm a unique D-U-N-S number, if you have yet to get one. It will proactively access the information required to build your company's profile. And it will contact the trade references that you have provided, in order to compute a current PAYDEX score for your firm.

D&B will incorporate approximately one hundred and fifty different factors into your company's credit file. These will be used to produce a Business Information Report, or BIR, which includes a full set of D&B scores and ratings.

D&B's fee for its CreditBuilder Plus program is $549.00, unless you purchase other services, in which case it is lower. The advantage of this fast-track process is that its own specialist staff takes the initiative to meet your goal.

Open credit files should also be registered with Equifax and Experian. You will have to supply the same basic information to these agencies.

Nobody but creditors can report payment experiences to the agencies. D&B is the only agency that will actively contact these firms, which it does under its CreditBuilder Plus program. If your suppliers don't report to Equifax or Experian, you will have to encourage them to do so. This will attest to your firm's all-important solid payment history, as reflected by the PAYDEX and DBT indices.

Each of the business credit bureaus routinely contact companies by telephone to update the basic data they have on file. The requested information on these calls is not up to the task of building the comprehensive credit profiles that you need.

Your credit profile will show public records, including any tax liens or judgments. You will want to settle and remove any unresolved issues, as soon as possible. They form a major black mark in the file.

Names of company officers are included in the reports. Also important, although not displayed there, are personal scores. Financial institutions want to know if you and other officers are credit worthy and will seek this information out. So it makes sense to understand what impacts your personal credit and do everything possible to build and maintain it, even though you and fellow officers do not want to be personally liable for the business credit that you seek.

If you or other officers are shown to have borrowed money with personal guarantees to invest in your business, this positively highlights your own confidence in its future.

Some people prefer to have their hands held through credit building process. Others decide to do the work themselves. It's not rocket science, but depends upon how urgently you want the job done. The key is to ensure that you provide everything needed to complete the comprehensive file. Also, that your creditors show that your firm pays its bills on time. You will want to work towards an excellent PAYDEX score of 80 or above with D&B, together with a low DBT with Equifax and Experian.

The Planned Outcome

If you have followed the steps outlined here, your company's credit profiles will gradually inspire additional confidence amongst trade suppliers, lenders and others.

It remains the right of any particular lender or supplier to ask you, or other officers, to sign a personal guarantee. But with better business credit you are in a much stronger position to either change suppliers, or to twist your current supplier's arm, to get what you want. After all, they will want to do business with a solid company, known to pay its bills promptly. And the record will show that yours fits the bill.

The benefit of good business credit is not limited to weaning yourself—and other officers—from reliance on personal guarantees. It also relates to better terms for insurance, leases and other supplies. This all boils down to increased personal asset protection, better cash flow and the potential to better leverage your company for growth. And what could be better than that?

Summary

1. Separate your personal credit from that of your company by building solid credit profiles with each of the three business credit agencies.

2. Follow the right steps to get greater access to revolving credit and better terms for other financing and supplies.

3. Personal risk is diminished when you reduce your personal assets to exposure.

Lesson

Become part of the small percentage of company owners who take positive steps to build and benefit from good business credit.

Additional Resource

BusinessCreditSuccess.com, founded by attorney Garrett Sutton and credit expert Gerri Detweiler, will show you how to build strong business credit and use it to your advantage.

15

Your Need for Good Systems

It's a fact that franchised businesses have a significantly lower failure rate than other startups. Why is this? It's likely because the prospective franchisee is forced to plan effectively for the venture. But also because franchises operate under standardized procedures and processes. These firms have to take a cookie-cutter approach to new operators and locations. There's no other way to do it.

I have worked with relatively few franchisees in the course of my work. Part of this is likely due to the fact that many of the problems that burden business can be attributed to operational chaos. In common with successful large firms, franchisers have to have these systems in place. It's the systems that eliminate this problem and characterize the franchise, or the large corporation.

If you don't have systems to handle each and every routine task, you're in for trouble. Michael Gerber, author of "The E-Myth," coined the term, "Work on your business, not in it." In other words, you are far better to take an arm's length look at the business and operate it from that viewpoint, than getting down and dirty with it, doing the routine technical stuff every day. If your business is totally dependent on you being there, then you've got a problem. Like the franchised operation, it has to depend on systems, not on your continued daily presence.

Gerber's observation that most small businesses are run by technicians, rather than managers, can rankle. It can seem counter-intuitive. After all, it hits at the commonly perceived notion of the entrepreneur as a free-spirited risk taker extraordinaire. But it is right on the mark. Any business that needs you to be there at all times is not a business—it's a job. That's not to say that it cannot meet your personal goals and be financially rewarding. It's just that it's not a business that you can grow or replicate. Or to sell at some point in the future, as a going concern.

What's a system?

We are talking about the written and understood process by which you manage your entire business, down to any particular task. Gerber likes to use the McDonald's analogy. Every new employee and franchise owner has to learn its management system. There's no way they're going to operate outside it. Everyone learns what to do and how to do it.

It involves every aspect of running the business, including greeting the customers, preparing the food, and cleaning the parking lot and washrooms. People have to learn the system, but are encouraged to make recommendations to improve upon it.

If you have good systems and maintain good control of them, you will maintain good control over your company. In other words, you give your employees the tools they need to consistently deliver the results you planned and need.

You have to ensure that your routine procedures are carried out in a standard way, the same way, every time. As a business owner you can quickly become bogged down, doing tasks that should be delegated to others. But how can they do this if there are no written standards or checklists in place?

Time is your most precious asset. You cannot develop your

time to manage and grow your business if you always have to be there—toiling away in the endless time-consuming routine.

How do systems work?

Simple processes form building blocks in your overall business system. Here are three examples, together with a fourth, which shows the need for one.

Restaurant

A small informal restaurant chain that I previously referred to had gotten into trouble after one of the locations became unprofitable. The company had not been set up properly to separate each restaurant as an independent corporation. A major problem at one location could sink the entire corporate ship.

A significant problem came to light when we did the turnaround. Whereas the same menu was used at each location, customers complained that there was no consistency between those at individual restaurants. A patron enjoying a submarine sandwich at one location would find that it tasted quite differently at another.

This wasn't the only issue. Customers were poorly greeted and escorted to their tables. There was a great deal of chaos and waste in the kitchen. Staff were confused about their respective responsibilities and reporting relationships.

The very first system the owner put in place was a standardized meal-preparation checklist. He ensured that the short-order cooks used the same ingredients and formula. This is a simple example, but it made a big difference to customer satisfaction.

The firm is still a long way behind having the kind of

systems you see in the casual dining chains such as T.G.I. Friday's or Bob Evans. But the owner saw the light and is on the right track.

By the way, doesn't it feel good to be cheerfully greeted by, "Welcome to Bob Evans," when you encounter the host in that chain restaurant? You can expect to be treated that way at each and every location—another simple example of a good system at work.

House painting

I recently worked with a large house painting business. The company had got into trouble from a series of external events, outside its control. But the owner had a system in place to track his advertising effectiveness. He knew, almost to the dollar, the response rate to advertising, per season and type of ad. We scrimped on other costs and ploughed every spare nickel into the most effective campaign, based on his careful tracking of past results.

This direct response system saved his company. We netted as much new business and cash as predicted. This brought in sufficient revenues to keep the lights on and the employees paid and, eventually, to resolve delinquent debt issues.

Commercial printing

Of all the business types I work with, commercial jobbing printers always seem to be the most chaotic. As I deal with companies in trouble, this may not typify the average printer. But you often walk in the front door and get the impression that everyone is harried.

Perhaps the place doesn't look too clean. The secretary has a hunted look on her face. And the stressed-out owner has a thousand things to do. He has little time to talk about pressing financial concerns before having to run out to lunch at the local business association. There, he wants to angle for new business and, incidentally, tell lies to his buddies about how well he is doing.

Philip Beyer (System100.com) knows this scenario all too well. He runs a Tennessee printing firm that he single-handedly transformed from chaos into an extraordinary business, by building simple step-by-step processes.

Beyer's approach derives from the E-Myth philosophy. His frustration drove his determination to fix his company, so he had a mental picture of what he was looking for. He then set out to systematically identify each and every key element of his business.

Beyer's book, "System Buster," details how he transformed his firm. It took him a few years to get there, and he did it the hard way—by figuring out how to do it by himself. He accomplished so much in his quest for an easily run, headache-free money machine that he felt compelled to let others profit from his experience.

Banking

I had a recent illustrative systems experience with a Philadelphia bank's legal counsel, who made a major mistake in a judgment filing. He filed against a firm that was well behind in its SBA loan commitments. Trouble was, the sum he claimed was about $400,000. This was double the approximately $200,000 it should have been. Even though the error went out over his signature, he unfairly blamed it on his assistant, whom he summarily fired.

The bank clearly did not have a system in place to verify that the information was correct, before the judgment was filed. All relevant officers should have checked such an important document for accuracy and signed off on it. Instead, this responsibility was left to the attorney, who in turn delegated the task to his unfortunate assistant.

You can bet your bottom dollar that the bank—and its legal counsel—has learned from the experience and put a relevant system in place. Had it been there at the outset, it would have—apart from anything else—saved the poor assistant's job and the attorney's waning reputation.

How do you get started?

You have possibly developed systems and checklists yourself, to manage individual processes as shown here. The ultimate aim is to get your business to the point where, like Philip Beyer's, it's a turnkey money machine.

To completely systematize your business, you can do everything yourself, or you can get professional help. I recommend the latter, because this is a situation in which you can use guidance and support in order to get the job done more easily.

The second printing of Beyer's publication, "System Busters: How to Stop Them in Your Business," is now available as a free eBook at System 100.com. As well, he now offers his proprietary software to businesses of all types. It is designed to help you to get your company's systems up and running in no time.

Michael Gerber's firm, E-Myth Worldwide, pioneered low cost, inexpensive "telecoaching" services. These sessions take a little time out of your busy schedule, but it is well spent.

Whatever route you take, effective business systems will yield the huge benefit of a simplified and proprietary way of managing your company. And what could be better than that?

Summary

1. Establish a systematic, proprietary way of doing business
2. This will free up your time and give you the lifestyle you dreamed of in the first place.

Lesson

Get help now to build your turnkey money machine.

16

How to get Paid—and Keep your Customer for Life

"You're a no-good deadbeat. Pay your bills." It was yet another objectionable collector on the line. My first business had encountered a major problem and I knew it. I was anxiously struggling to bring in revenues, but I didn't need this.

"Excuse me?" I countered. "Why don't you come to my place of business? Then you can stand in front of me and repeat what you just said." Thoughts of paying the creditor disappeared for the moment, supplanted by visions of thumping the SOB collector.

Things were getting out of hand when collectors felt justified in speaking to me in that way—albeit from the safety of a distant cubicle. But I couldn't permit myself to become overly affected by these tactics. If anything, I realized that they were counterproductive to both sides. I knew that I was not the only entrepreneur struggling to survive. Nobody else would want to be spoken to in that way. And I became convinced that there had to be a better way for creditors to get paid, while keeping the customer, than to hire the type of telephonic goon that was calling my business.

This all took place in the early 1990's. In dealing with collectors today, as an agent of debtor firms, I find them generally more professional. I think it has sunk in that they get more cooperation, and payments, by taking a more conciliatory approach. But my personal experience colored my thinking. I knew that there had to be a better way to maximize collection of delinquent receivables while reconciling the needs of both parties. And there is.

The Importance of Credit

My Barber gets paid in cash, on time, every time he gives service. If you don't have the green stuff, you don't go to see him. No invoices, receivables or collection calls. George is a happy guy and a constant source of humor. I suspect it's got to do with his payment terms. But I bet he'd lose his smile if you told him, post-trim, that you couldn't pay.

Better yet is to get money up front. Cash on the barrel, before delivery. It avoids the prospect of the customer starting to negotiate new terms following receipt of your goods or services.

The Hooker Principle illustrates this situation. That is, the client's perceived monetary value of goods or services takes a nosedive right after their receipt. In other words, it's best to get paid up front, when the desire is strong. It's all downhill after that. George wields sharp instruments, and is satisfied with his present arrangements, thank you.

Cash deals are nice for the seller, but in the real world of business-to-business commerce, most firms just have to extend credit. This is a risky investment in your customer. Cash flow, not receivables, is your life-blood. It is frustrating not to get paid as agreed. But it can be short sighted to look at any particular receivable in isolation because, handled properly, it represents a future stream of income from a paying, satisfied customer.

My own experience and comments here relate primarily to business-to-business transactions. Accounts receivable make up about forty percent of the assets of most of the businesses I deal with. That's a heck of a lot of money tied up in other people's hands. It means that return on your capital may be less important that return <u>of</u> your capital. There is significant risk inherent in handing its control to others. So it goes without saying that accounts receivable management is crucially important to your company.

Your collections function is an extension of sales, where customer service is paramount. It was sales and marketing that got you the account in the first place. And the integrated process is all about good communication, aimed at safeguarding your company's valuable assets and its base of future income.

Seen rationally, your goal is to maximize the benefit received now, as well as in future, from each and every account. If you want to continue to do productive business with a particular late-paying firm, you have to understand its reasons for extreme tardiness. The vast majority of business managers and consumers are good, honest individuals like you, and the exception proves the rule.

How do you collect late receivables?

The conventional collections approach varies by industry, but generally assumes that you must immediate take strong measures to collect a past-due account. Standard advice, after in-house attempts have failed, is to refer past-due payables to an agency. But will that really meet your joint goals of account collection and long-term customer value? The conventional collection agency approach is expensive, not very effective and alienates customers.

The collector is certainly motivated to earn a commission of up to fifty per cent for his firm by collecting the sum due. But he has absolutely no interest in your future relationship with that customer.

My own experience is different. Business owners who are unable to keep current with payables tend to be highly uncomfortable. They don't like to be in that position. And they hate to have to admit their situation to their creditors. The account remains unpaid for the simple reason that they are short of cash. The trouble is, you don't know it because they haven't told you. All you know is that, for whatever reason, your firm has not received payment on this overdue account.

You won't be effective with a blanket policy of treating all your late payers as adversaries, or by retaining a proudly aggressive collection agency to threaten and cajole them. It took your sales people precious time and money to win these accounts in the first place. It doesn't make sense to throw them out with the bath water.

Psychological factors come into play when accounts remain unpaid, especially when you deal with smaller firms. It takes little to start a confrontation with defensive individuals, who may then come up with a myriad of internal justifications for not paying as agreed. Unless handled well, the situation will deteriorate. To use the terminology of Dale Carnegie, the best way to win an argument is to avoid it.

Whatever steps you take, you have to act quickly, as experience shows that the older the receivable, the less likely you are to get paid. Recent Commercial Law League of America data points to an average recovery of little more than seventy-three per cent at three months past due. This plummets to barely ten per cent at twenty-four months. Companies close down and disappear.

Start off right with new accounts

Time and again, I see companies granted credit when they have been nothing but trouble to other vendors. For whatever reason, their credit references were never checked out with others in your industry. Or the creditor was so desperate for business that it hoped for the best. This is not wise. A few potential customers may be dishonest and unethical. They will lose you money. Don't deal with them.

As a rule, rigorously check references. This is one time when you do to people what you don't want done to you. Tie them up with personal guarantees, especially if you have any reservations about dealing with them. It is much easier to get paid, when push comes to shove, when you have two corporate officers and possibly a spouse encumbered in this way. And if they have bad references and don't want to do that, don't get yourself into trouble by dealing with them.

Sales people will often have a handle on which customers are doing poorly. They can ferret out trouble at an early stage. But you have to make sure that they are working in your firm's best interests. It makes no sense for them to turn down sales unless you have a process in place to tie commission and bonuses to your firm's ability to collect.

The ideal solution—Pre-arranged settlements

My own experience in dealing with troubled companies is that most of them are managed honestly. They are empathetic, to a fault, with the needs of their creditors. After all, they probably have personal experience in trying to collect their own late receivables. And it follows that it can be counter-productive to threaten them. Business people respond well to those who understand their situation and help with the root cause of their financial problems. They don't want to be treated like the tiny percent of business owners who want to find a way to avoid addressing the problem.

Given that the predominant issue is financial ability, if you could wave a magic wand and improve your debtor firms' economic outlook they would be willing and able to pay their bills. In our experience, it makes sense for the creditor to take steps to establish the reasons for late-payment before deciding how to proceed.

If there is a legitimate contractual complaint, you can identify and deal with it directly. In the more likely event that it is a financial issue, impacting all of the debtor firm's creditors, you can tackle it in a way in which is proven to be highly successful. This is to help the firm manage its way through the problem. Collectors don't do this. But if you become sure that the debtor is being evasive or dishonest, you can refer the matter to an attorney for conventional legal remedies.

Setting up the Process

It is good policy to retain a debt management specialist for this purpose. That person would consult with you, free of charge, to work out a pre-arranged discounted cash settlement for each and every delinquent account. Remember that a collector will charge up to fifty percent on any sum collected. Your aim is twofold. You want to:

- Equal or better the net amount that you would receive from a collector, and
- Maximize lifetime customer value by retaining the account in the long term

The specialist then approaches your customer to offer this proposal in a non-confrontational manner. Payment would have to be made by a specific date. The debt manager doesn't stop there. He gives that firm the opportunity to improve its overall financial situation. The consulting fee charged the debtor firm is a percentage of the savings achieved on its delinquent accounts.

Your Benefits

The net result is that:

- You will likely receive the planned discounted amount of your delinquent account(s) in short order.

- Your customer will be indebted to you for your enlightened, helpful approach and for the cost savings, which went to his firm rather than to a collector.

- Your customer will, with the assistance of the professional help you have referred, be more likely to get back on track.

- Perhaps best of all, you keep a paying customer with a more resilient business. It will be committed to purchasing from you for years to come, if on revised credit terms in the short term.

This pre-arranged settlement process is outlined in Exhibit #10 and works with all of your delinquent commercial accounts. By doing your due diligence in this way, you tactfully identify those who have real financial problems and need help. And the typically small percentage of firms that refuse to pay for whatever reason can be earmarked for immediate legal action.

Exhibit #10

Pre-Arrangement Settlement Process

1. Establish the dollar amount that you would accept for each and every delinquent receivable on your list of receivables, if you would be able to receive these funds either immediately, or within a specific short time frame. Each sum is based on your firm's immediate cash needs and expectations and the projected lifetime value of the account.

2. Engage the services of a debt management professional to review your goals and to work towards them, at no cost to you.

3. The debt manager discreetly and tactfully approaches your debtor firms. The intent is to systematically address outstanding payables problems within these firms and to:
   a. prioritize payment of your particular account,
   b. at the discount you pre-arranged,
   c. within your specified time frame.

4. If necessary, the debt manager liasises with you to review and revise payment arrangements.

5. Upon documented agreement, execured by each party, debtor firm submits funds to:
   a. You, as creditor, for the pre-arranged settlement, and
   b. the debt manager, for the results-based fee.

If you are unable to find someone to do this work, contact my office by fax at 302-765-2516 or email at results@biz911.com. We will either help you directly or forward information on how to get started with a debt management professional.

Summary

1. Past-due receivables can force you out of business, unless you manage your collections process effectively. Unfortunately, this happens all too often. Set your company apart and communicate clearly and effectively with your delinquent accounts.

2. Minimize your risks when taking on new customers by using appropriate credit granting guidelines. It is also crucial to maintain close contact with your sales and marketing staff and with credit managers in other firms in your industry. Sales people will often have a good idea of those customers who represent an evolving credit risk, as may your counterparts in other firms.

3. Above all, treat those responsible for your past-due accounts with respect, even the few that may prove themselves unworthy of it. If this courtesy is not reciprocated, bring in the heavy guns and take them to court. If it takes this to get paid, so be it. You might lose any future business from that particular account, but you are likely better off without it.

4. The net result of this approach is that you will get paid more now, and in overall lifetime value, from your currently delinquent customers.

Lesson

Benefit from an enlightened collections process, geared to assist past-due customers in financial trouble and maintaining their future business. Assign other accounts to the collection attorney for quick results.

AFTERWORD

Few things in life are more satisfying than helping a good company to stem its losses, recoup and get back on track. Creditors get paid much more than if it had gone out of business. Jobs and marriages are saved, while the corporate officers and company emerge with a new resilience.

For a business in financial trouble, the ideal is for it to immediately get out of danger solely by reorganizing and changing its sales and marketing strategy. Unfortunately, a quick fix is not always possible. Circumstances differ, but positive steps can be difficult and options limited when cash is scarce and the wolves are howling at the door. This is why the strategies outlined in Part One are so important.

The best business people are adept at managing crises. In fact, this may be the most important success characteristic of all because everyone fails somewhere along the line. The more successful you are as an individual, the more failures you are likely to have under your belt. The key is to be able to do what it takes to help your business survive and forge its way to the next level.

In my experience, communication is the key. It needs to be part of your company's culture. As we have discussed, good internal systems are paramount. And when trouble hits, the same applies to dealings with creditors of all stripes. Nobody likes unpleasant surprises. But it becomes much worse for the creditor, be they banker, landlord or goods and services supplier, when they come to believe that wool is being pulled over their eyes. It is easy for them to think this when they are not getting paid as agreed and they can't get straight answers.

We all—creditors and debtors alike—want to be treated with honesty, courtesy and integrity. This makes all the difference when working your way through a business turnaround. Take Dale Carnegie's advice and give potential adversaries a good reputation to live up to. Don't become defensive and argue with them, even if they are that way with you. Chances are, they will appreciate your approach and react accordingly.

I hope you find this book enjoyable and informative. I wish you the best of success and look forward to your feedback and questions. I want to go the extra mile for you, my valued reader. If you have any comments or questions, please feel free to get in touch by fax at 302-765-2516, or email at results@biz911.com.

ABOUT THE AUTHOR

Ken Thomson is the president of Biz911, Inc. This Delaware-based firm helps good small-to-medium sized firms to hurdle tough debt problems and prevail. The corporate name reflects the emergency response nature of the company's work. It was in use years before the 9/11 tragedy in New York and the association of 911 with that event.

Ken takes great pride in the fact that his company has proactively helped many hundreds of businesses throughout the U.S. to survive and prosper. A University of Wisconsin-Madison graduate, his post-graduate degrees from the University of London and Queen's University, Canada, are in agricultural business and public administration. His real education, however, has been in the down-and-dirty practicalities of business crisis management, starting with his own first major endeavor. It was this trial-by-fire that led him to realize how lonely and isolated an entrepreneur can feel when in trouble.

Biz911's results-oriented services address client needs to get well out of danger. Unmanageable debt is resolved. Proven, cost-effective business development strategies boost revenues. This puts them on the right track—poised to become the resilient turnkey money machines they were meant to be in the first place.

INDEX